"Debbie Ford was a spiritual sister, colleague, and teacher to me. This book, discovered after her passing, is an extraordinary journey to higher consciousness. Read it, absorb her insights, and you may see the world as fresh, vibrant, and holy as if for the first time."

—DEEPAK CHOPRA

"Debbie Ford was and is one of the greatest teachers of my lifetime. Not only did she evolve, modernize, and render accessible the concept of shadow work and wholeness . . . but she was/is also one of the most profound spiritual teachers of our time. I am so happy that this book was written and will be shared with the world. May this book serve as the gift that it is, from the deeply empathic and wise soul that she was and is."

—ALANIS MORISSETTE

"'You are a holy addition to this world.' Do you believe that? If you do (with all your heart or halfheartedly), but especially if you don't believe it at all, put this book on your bedside table and read little bits of it every night before you sleep, and every morning when you awaken. Its beauty and truth will seep into your consciousness and fill you with faith and strength. Debbie left us too soon, but she left a trail of light, and she left this book."

—ELIZABETH LESSER,
cofounder of Omega Institute

"Truly a remarkable angel, who has brought the mindset of *God, prayer,* and *love* into a form of daily worship for your soul. I have known Debbie in her human life and spirit life and she insisted to me that this book be published. Use this book and open yourself to the light and compassion of the heavens."

—JAMES VAN PRAAGH,
bestselling author and master medium

"Debbie Ford is one of the wisest, most insightful, most gentle and loving people I have ever had the joy of calling 'friend.' My life—like the lives of so many, many others—has been deeply enriched by her. And now, it is enriched again by the offering of these gifts from her mind to ours, shared with us even after she has celebrated her Continuation Day, and opening us to what could be the most powerful tool that has ever been placed in our hands by God. Thank you, Sweet Friend, for one more timeless treasure."

—NEALE DONALD WALSCH,
bestselling author of *Conversations with God*

"Debbie was a colleague and dear friend and she is missed by all who knew her and her work. *Your Holiness* is a treasure newly unearthed to be shared by all who are riddled by fear and anxiety. There is a powerful force that exists within each of us. We can sense its potential, but harnessing it can feel like a lifetime of work. In this timeless and important work, Debbie Ford fearlessly uncovers this light within and in so doing reveals a path to our higher selves. This 'holy shift in consciousness,' as Debbie calls it, is right there for all seeking unshakable strength and love."

—JUDITH ORLOFF,
New York Times bestselling author of *Emotional Freedom*

"When I met Debbie Ford six months before she died, we fell into friendship-smitten-love immediately. I loved her honesty, her humor, and her willingness to reveal the dark side of anything while simultaneously holding its light. It's such a joy to be with her all over again through *Your Holiness*—and to be reminded that everything we think we want out there is already ours for the asking, for the looking, for the willingness to receive. A heavenly message indeed."

—GENEEN ROTH,
author of *Women Food and God* and *Lost and Found*

"*Your Holiness* is a beautiful, evocative, honest, and heartfelt offering from the late Debbie Ford—coach, trailblazer, truth-teller, and courageous leader. Towards the end of her life I was fortunate to get to know her intimately and call her my friend. The Debbie I remember, in the many conversations we had over the years, was to me a deeply spiritual person, unafraid of sharing this side of her life. I am so grateful to yet again be able to embrace this most important part of her and hear her voice again, if even from the pages of a book. Finally, with such a beautiful book in our hands, we all can now witness and celebrate all the aspects of this extraordinary woman's truest legacy. If you are tired of surfing the dark side, this book will lift you up and show you where the miracles are hidden in plain sight. *Your Holiness* is a classic and will still be relevant in years to come."

—COLETTE BARON-REID,
bestselling author, spiritual medium, and founder of Oracle School®

"*Your Holiness* is a rare gift, filled with the wisdom we all need to be our best selves today. This 'found' manuscript by my dear friend Debbie Ford is an urgent message and a guide to access the holiness we each have inside. This hidden power is the key to happiness and the life we all desire."

—MARCI SHIMOFF,
New York Times bestselling author of *Happy for No Reason*

"Leave it to my dear friend Debbie Ford to bless us with her wisdom several years after she left for the other side of the veil. I knew she had more wisdom and grace to offer us, and this book is the proof. It was written before she passed and contains many of the prayers that lifted her life above the struggles many of us encounter. It is the demonstration of a life dedicated to service, a life that continues to bless those of us who love her."

—JAMES TWYMAN,
New York Times bestselling author and Peace Troubadour

"During her all-too-brief time on earth, Debbie Ford lived through an extraordinary range of human experience and shared with us the exquisitely wise, healing revelations of her own Higher Self. Now, in *Your Holiness,* she reminds us that her glorious Heart is still with us. In what may be her most significant gift to humanity, she shows us— with crystal clear insight, and straightforward, practical suggestions—how to access our Higher Self . . . How to turn our lives over to the Higher Power we all long to love, and serve . . . and how to truly *feel* its 'holiness' vibrating in and around us in every moment of every day. This book is a great, great blessing for all who read it—a magnificent guidebook for the spiritual journey."

—RAMANANDA JOHN E. WELSHONS,
author of *One Soul, One Love, One Heart* and *Awakening from Grief*

"This book is a miracle. It is drenched with all of Debbie Ford's magic and wisdom that brings you right back into your soul. She is forever teaching us from the heavens."

—LIZ DAWN,
CEO of Celebrate Your Life Events

"Everyone should read this book! It not only helps you here in the physical world, but also helps to infuse and empower your soul through the grace and power of prayer!"

—JOHN HOLLAND,
spiritual medium and teacher

"How fortunate for us that Debbie's tenacious teaching and seeking spirit revealed this found treasure she left behind. *Your Holiness* is an exquisite guide into the divine depth of healing and love available inside each one of us when we allow ourselves to be a channel for grace. This book is an oracle; let each page empower you to recognize and honor the truth of your heart and soul."

—NANCY LEVIN,
bestselling author of *Worthy*

"Debbie understood that the true power of prayer was not to stand in your current place waiting to receive a free handout, but to be actively involved in partnering with G-d by creating the blessings and joy of our highest, deepest potential. She had huge wings of love and awe of her creator, which she skillfully used to propel her ascent through her ladder of prayer. Her overflowing heart of kindness wanted nothing more in this life than to be able to pin those wings onto the backs of anyone courageous enough to join her march."

—RABBI BARUCH EZAGUI,
director of Chabad of La Jolla

"Debbie Ford's *Your Holiness* is clearly an offering directly from her spirit, an invitation to tenderly embrace and surrender ourselves to the higher self with the utmost trust that Grace is our constant companion. Read this book and then read it again, letting its compassionate teachings wash over you and bless your life."

—MICHAEL BERNARD BECKWITH,
author of *Spiritual Liberation*

"This book is a pathway to the possibility of a great life through great choices that can be found through the amazing power of authentic prayer. Read this, not only once for inspiration—read this daily, for a new breath of life."

—MARY MORRISSEY,
author of *The Miracle Minute*

"Debbie Ford has done it again. *Your Holiness* is filled with so much grace it makes me weep deep tears of gratitude for her profound words. This book will remain on my bookshelf as long as there is breath in my body."

—MADISYN TAYLOR,
bestselling author of the DailyOM book series

"In this soulful book, Debbie leads us on an unforgettable journey that opens our hearts to a more empowering life, filled with grace. Struggling with drug addiction, Debbie was led on a journey to find her connection to her inner world, her true essence which liberated her from suffering. Going within, Debbie discovered that connecting with Source, the God that is in each of us, is the catalyst that heals us and releases us from bondage. Not only is this a deep and insightful book, but within its pages, it is revealed how to make dramatic shifts in our own consciousness, to make life work, and return to our most magnificent self, our holiness."

—ANITA MOORJANI,
New York Times bestselling author of *Dying to Be Me*

"In the scriptures of the Upanishads we are told that everything in the universe is pervaded by the Divine. Everything and everyone is holy and divine. To really and experientially know that truth is enlightenment. Through this beautiful book, Debbie transmits this sacred truth in a way that is understandable, meaningful, applicable, and implementable for readers of every walk of life and every spiritual background. In a simple and compelling way, she provides the 'master key' to unlock all the doors of our hearts, our minds, and our lives."

—SADHVI BHAGAWATI SARASWATIJI,
president of Divine Shakti Foundation

"*Your Holiness* is an answered prayer: the chance to once again sit and listen to Debbie as she shares her most powerful wisdom and teachings. Her final book is a beautiful love letter to humanity: an invitation to cherish yourself, to claim your divinity, and to create an unbreakable bond with God that will allow you to step fully into the life you are meant to live. From the first page to the last, Debbie reminds us that all transformation begins and ends with love. Read this book slowly, carefully, and let its beauty and inspired Grace seep into your bones. It will change you. It changed me. Bless you, Debbie Ford."

—CHERYL RICHARDSON,
bestselling author of *Take Time for Your Life*

YOUR HOLINESS

YOUR HOLINESS

Discover the Light Within

DEBBIE FORD

HAY HOUSE

Carlsbad, California • New York City • London
Sydney •Johannesburg • Vancouver • New Delhi

First published and distributed in the United States of America by:
HarperCollins Publishers, 195 Broadway, New York, NY 10007

First published and distributed in the United Kingdom by:
Hay House UK Ltd, Astley House, 33 Notting Hill Gate, London W11 3JQ
Tel: +44 (0)20 3675 2450; Fax: +44 (0)20 3675 2451; www.hayhouse.co.uk

Published and distributed in Australia by:
Hay House Australia Ltd, 18/36 Ralph St, Alexandria NSW 2015
Tel: (61) 2 9669 4299; Fax: (61) 2 9669 4144; www.hayhouse.com.au

A catalogue record for this book is available from the British Library.

ISBN: 978-1-78817-144-1

Printed and bound in Great Britain by TJ International, Padstow, Cornwall.

For my beautiful mother, Sheila,
who has always been my biggest champion.
I love you.

CONTENTS

SECTION THREE | The Holy Cleanse

SECTION FOUR | Healing Your Whole Heart

SECTION FIVE | Holy Medicine

SECTION SIX | Reclaiming Your Light

FOREWORD

My sister, the late, great, amazing Debbie Ford, was a *New York Times* bestselling author of ten books who had dedicated her life to her global community of students and coaches, teaching her groundbreaking work on "the shadow" and innovating the life-changing Shadow Process Workshop. Along with raising her son, Beau, her work was her greatest passion and focus. During the last five years of her life, as she courageously dealt with a rare cancer, she found the will and strength to get out of bed and teach for a week and then would collapse for a month to rest up and generate enough energy to do it again.

Now that Debbie is on the other side, her tremendous desire to serve humanity has not slowed down. Whether you believe in an afterlife or not, I continue to receive emails, phone calls, and social media messages on a near daily basis from her friends, students, and coaches and even strangers sharing with me that Debbie is guiding them from the other side via dreams, direct messages, and signs. Her presence after her death with those who are living has made itself known in so many ways. We don't expect this to stop, especially given this incredible account.

A longtime family friend, celebrated medium, and close confidant of Debbie's, James Van Praagh, sent an invitation for a private reading to my husband (Brian) and me, together with my mom, Sheila. We were to visit his new home, located less than forty-five minutes from us, and he would provide a reading with

Debbie and other deceased relatives who were willing to come through time and space to meet with us. Of course—without hesitation—we all said yes. (These days, if you want a reading with James you have to attend his public events—where there are often three thousand people or more—and hope your loved one on the other side is pushy enough to grab his attention.)

On a beautiful, warm, sunny Monday afternoon the week before Christmas, we drove to James's beautiful home north of San Diego. After a tour of his serene, personal paradise, we got comfortable in his very white and extremely modern office. He began the session. All of us were so excited to hear who would come through as well as experience the gifts of our dear friend James.

Within seconds, Debbie spoke through James with a request for me to write a prayer book with her. It was as if she had been waiting to announce this request for some time. She made a case for how she would help me through the entire process. It could be fun and easy, she said. I didn't understand what she was talking about and was cringing with every detail. How would this be possible? Would I have to impose on James for daily readings to get the material? I said no as politely as you could to a sister who has passed away. Debbie eventually moved on to other topics.

Next James asked us, "Who is Minnie? She keeps talking about Minnie."

I explained that Minnie is Beau's half sister (who almost no one knows about . . . you can't even Google that information).

"Ah, now I get it," James said. "She says to tell Beau that when Minnie was visiting recently, she was with them every precious moment."

Geez, how did James know that Minnie had come to visit

Beau for Thanksgiving (from her home in London) just a few weeks prior?

"Damn," I thought. This guy is beyond good; he's truly a master. It seems like the entire cosmos comes through this kind and gentle man.

The reading progressed and Brian's parents came through with sweet messages; my stepfather, Doc, came through, which made my mother incredibly happy; and a few other deceased relatives came through who had valuable messages to share.

In between visits from the other loved ones, Debbie would break through, continuing to implore me to write a prayer book with her. I had tried to say no, but apparently social etiquette is different for the dead. By the end of our ninety-minute session, I caved in and said yes. Clueless as to how it would happen, I knew my sister well enough that she would never let this go until I agreed. It was hard to believe that even from the other side she could still boss me around! Persistence is her middle name.

As we drove home on the freeway later that day, Brian began talking about all the many meaningful and cherished hours he spent with Debbie at her chemo treatments. He had memories of her talking about writing prayers over the years. He remembered how important they were to her, and he suggested that I contact Julie to see what she might know.

Julie, in addition to being someone we consider family, was and is a vast resource of all things Debbie. She spent seven years working as Debbie's right hand and held titles that included executive assistant, producer, webmaster, editorial assistant, business manager, and collaborator on many projects. At the end of Debbie's life, Julie was her primary caregiver and gave of herself tirelessly to make sure Debbie's every need was taken care of. The love and strong bond between them was a joy and an honor to witness. Today, she continues Debbie's legacy as president and chief operating officer of The Ford Institute.

I called Julie and shared the details of the reading. I finished the story, and Julie was not surprised in the least. Her response floored me:

"Arielle, Debbie wrote an entire prayer book called *Your Holiness*. Do you want me to send the manuscript to you?"

Within minutes, I was reading the book you now hold in your hands. I was mesmerized. I had completely forgotten that the catalyst for Debbie's total lifesaving transformation from a life of using hard drugs was the extraordinary power of prayer. I had forgotten that nearly thirty years before she passed on, she had fallen in love with God and that she had experienced a true miracle thanks to prayer. As I read each page, my heart continued to expand, and I felt as if Debbie was with me, enjoying each prayer together. Her words leaped off the page, and I could feel her loving energy all around me, her frequency enveloping me with such a comforting presence.

Not only was the book brilliant and beautifully written, it was complete. The book was never published; perhaps Debbie felt the time was not right until now.

I realized immediately how divine the timing of all this was and how many hearts and minds this book would touch. And, of course, I was delighted that I wouldn't have to figure out how to coauthor a book with an angel from the other side. Debbie wanted me to help be the messenger.

When I finished reading, I picked up the phone and called Gideon Weil at HarperOne. I told him about the extraordinary reading with James and the manuscript I held in my hands. He had been Debbie's editor for many years; he is also my editor and James Van Praagh's editor. No coincidences here.

After listening to this crazy story, Gideon admitted—to my astonishment—that he had been feeling guilty for the past few years. Debbie wrestled balancing her hard-hitting psychological insights with a desire to write more about spirituality and how each of us has a divine self. Gideon eventually persuaded Debbie to "stay in her lane" and focus on what she was best known for—the psychological. Debbie, of course, has never given up, and apparently she believes the moment to flex her spiritual insights is now. I sent him the manuscript, and within days he agreed to publish it.

You just can't make this stuff up: sometimes it's just better to surrender to the magic and grace of this thing called life.

As the end of her precious life approached, Debbie told me she was completely satisfied that her mission was fulfilled, that she had experienced a great life, and that the last year of her life, despite her weakened condition and constant pain, had been the best year of her life. It's exciting to have proof that even from her new home in heaven she continues to share her deep wisdom.

Debbie's love and affinity for prayer carried her through some of the darkest moments of her life. I am beyond thrilled that she found a way to let us know this book existed and that in doing so, her inspiring words are now available to lift and enlighten the rest of us. I hope you enjoy this book as much as we enjoyed the adventure of uncovering this treasure.

ARIELLE FORD
La Jolla, California

INTRODUCTION

In science, technology, medicine, business, or almost any other corner of human invention, there is always new information being discovered.

When it comes to spirituality, however, there is never new information discovered so much as new insight gleaned from information we already have. The great spiritual avatars and source materials have articulated the great religious truths; the journey of consciousness is humanity's evolving to the point of embodying what we know.

The scientist and the spiritual teacher, therefore, are different not only in what they reveal externally but in what they reveal internally. While who a scientist is has little to do with the import of his or her scientific discovery, who the spiritual transmitter is has everything to do with the depth of his or her transmission. When it comes to information of the soul, only one who him- or herself has truly been *in-formed* can pass along spiritual information beyond a mere sharing of abstract concepts. What makes *Your Holiness* such a beautiful book is not only what Debbie Ford wrote on the page, but also the obvious depths from which she wrote it.

To those of us who knew Debbie as a vibrant, generous, courageous woman, it is hard to read these words without some level of sorrow that she isn't here to see them published. On the other hand, the book itself is a reminder of a greater reality than that of the material plane, a reality of which we are all a part and through which the spirit remains alive forever. Debbie found her own comfort and healing in aligning with that reality, and one of her greatest gifts to the world while she was here was to remind us all that such a power exists.

In this book, she does more than simply remind us. In these pages she wrote of more than God's existence, or even of his power; she wrote of how to *experience* that power by practicing the authentic steps of spiritual transformation: prayer, forgiveness, and humility before God.

Debbie did not pretend that she hadn't fallen down in life, or that she alone had lifted herself back up. Rather, she was brutally honest with herself and others about her problems—the demonic, addictive forces that had laid her flat on the ground and threatened to destroy her life. And she wrote beautifully about the moments of surrender through which she felt God had lifted her back up.

Realizing the depth of the drug hell into which she had descended, she wrote that more than anything else at that time, she wanted to change. She wanted to stop living the lie she knew she was living. Lying desperate on the cold tiles of a bathroom floor at the height of her madness, she called out to God in the midst of her pain:

> *I wanted to change. I needed to change so badly. I began begging and crying hysterically. With my head in my hands, I sobbed uncontrollably until I suddenly realized that something inside me had shifted. A calm had come over me—a silence that was palpable. In asking God, this higher power, to enter my awareness, something inside me opened up and relaxed. The stress in my body had released, and the screaming voice in my mind had subsided. Peace had enveloped my entire self. Even the filthy, disgusting*

bathroom floor didn't look so bad. There was a release inside me, a letting go, a clarity, an expansiveness, but more importantly, there was hope. My God, I had hope. Just what I needed.

That hope was not what just Debbie needed; it's a hope that we all need. Today, her message has particular poignancy for those bound in the hell of drug addiction like she was, many of whom die all too frequently on those same dirty floors. Yet most of us, whatever the form of our darkness, can relate to the pain of a life gone wrong.

Debbie lived the human journey of having been to hell and back, then shared with her audiences how God had done for her what she couldn't do for herself. If even one person reads this book and embraces the thought that "If God would restore Debbie to new life, then perhaps he will do it for me, too," then she will have given a gift in this lifetime that makes her worthy of our eternal gratitude.

What had Debbie done that day, the one key she had never used before but which at that moment made all the difference? What made that the day the clouds broke through at last?

That day, she prayed. She completely surrendered her life to God.

As an addict, Debbie learned that no amount of self-will or self-discipline was strong enough to lift her above the ever-recurring temptations to drag her life back into the downward spiral that had haunted her for years. She would go on to develop not just a life of prayer but a true devotee's understanding of its effects that she now delivers to others for their own healing.

The fruits of her labor are in your hands.

"Prayer is the path that delivers us to our most divine selves," she wrote.

It washes us clean and tills the soil of our consciousness so that more life-affirming, holy thoughts and feelings can take root. When we are in the presence of our power, potential, beauty, worthiness, and light, we are not as vulnerable to critical thoughts of despair, self-doubt, greed, fear, blame, or darkness. When we are connected to our spiritual essence, we feel good enough, wanted, loved, confident, safe, and inspired. And when we are disconnected, we feel scared, small, weak, unworthy, unlovable, abandoned, and alone. As Emmet Fox once said in The Golden Key, *"If you are thinking about your difficulty, you are not thinking about God." Through the vehicle of prayer, we come to know God. Through the power of prayer, we come to know our holiness.*

Debbie realized, from bitter experience, that only the light of her holiness could keep her safe and protected from the darkness of her ego mind. She was clear that an alignment with the holiness in which we were all created was and is the greatest, most meaningful, and most important pursuit of our lives.

"What does it take to step into and reclaim your holiness? I'm going to assert that it is much easier than you might imagine," she wrote. "Most of us think we have to become something, learn something, succeed at something, or achieve something, but in truth the realization of our holiest self requires nothing from the outer world. Stepping into our holiness is merely a process of acceptance, of being willing to see the totality of ourselves. It is the recognition of the magnificence and grandness of our own potential."

Yet Debbie never sugarcoated the journey that it takes to reach our grand potential. She was never blind to the difficulties or the challenges that go along with spiritual pursuit. There is no holiness without love, and love is not always easy. We must face the places where we hold lovelessness within our consciousness, and we must root it out; until then, we will always be vulnerable to the toxicity of a spiritually inauthentic existence. Naming steps to the dissolution of our lovelessness, she calls in this book for a Consciousness Cleanse:

> *You must . . . acknowledge that you have allowed thoughts and feelings that are inconsistent with the vibration of love into the sacred environment of your mind, body, and heart. You must admit that you consciously and unconsciously, intentionally and unintentionally, opened up to these frequencies, and you chose to interpret some of your experiences in negative ways, which is what made them toxic to you. It's important to realize that your interpretations of your life's events are what make them nourishing or toxic.*

Debbie was rigorous in her approach to spiritual growth, and she urges the reader to be rigorous as well. She knew from experience that her thoughts could bring her down, and she knew that only thoughts of God could bring her back up. Moreover, she knew that only she could choose which thoughts to hold within her mind. When she chose holiness, the power of her faith created an anti-gravitational pull that overrode all lower forces.

> *You are the only one who can choose. You are as free to change vibrational frequencies as you are to change your clothes. Your thoughts, your emotions, the images you hold in your mind, the energetic signals that you send out to all those around you—these are the tools that are*

available to you in this life experience. Use them to your
full advantage. Do not for one more minute deny your
holiness, your godliness, and the power of your true self.
Because you are wanted, needed, and, more importantly, a
holy addition to this world. So open up, commit, and enjoy
this journey, your holy ride.

Debbie did rise up from the depths of her drug-induced despair that day, and she did in time enjoy her ride. She became a successful teacher, author, and coach, living happily a life filled with love and abundance.

Even then, though, it wasn't as though she didn't face life's challenges. The idea of one or two eureka moments and then everything is perfect from that point forward didn't hold true for Debbie and doesn't hold true for any of us. She wrote honestly of the lies and prejudices that all of us are heir to while living in a space so permeated by the illusions of the world.

Alignment with our holiness doesn't mean all the sorrow of life then ends, but it does mean the sorrows of life become bearable. What we gain from an experience of holiness is a set of new eyes through which to view heartaches, and the spiritual strength to rise above them:

In the midst of life's heartaches, we must find the eyes to
see beyond our current situation. The fact remains that we
are going to have tough times. People are going to die. We
are going to lose love. We are going to struggle. We can
pray until we are blue in the face for things to be different,
but most of the time we are powerless to stop heartache,
because it is an inevitable part of life. Creation and
destruction, life and death, good times and bad times . . .
If you have a father who is riddled with cancer, there is a

99 percent chance that he is going to die. Praying for him not to, although you could do it, is a prayer that you can't expect God to answer. But what you can pray for, what you do have influence over, is for you to be the strongest, most centered and loving person possible during those times. You can pray for the courage to love through your fear, to allow love in through other sources. You can pray for enough love in your heart so you can grieve in a healthy way. You can pray for your loved one to find comfort, to have faith, to have an easy passing. What you do have the power over, what you do need, is the understanding that this is life, that this too shall pass, and that an all-loving grace is with you and supports you in transcending the moment, enabling you to see beyond your current circumstances. The mantra "This too shall pass" lifts your consciousness so you can look at your life five days or five months out and know that you're going to be okay.

Debbie's triumph lay not in a long life but in a meaningful life, for herself and for many others. She died way too young from the perspective of those who greedily would have wished to have her with us longer. Yet the life she lived was one of inspiration to so many, and with this book she continues to give of her spiritual bounty. Her inspiration seemed boundless, yet with characteristic generosity she insisted it was a gift that is available to all.

Inspiration is magical, ever-present, and unlimited— you only have to tap into it. You don't have to become inspired. You are inspired. Beyond all limitations of human life, inspiration is the emanating force of the universe. It lives vibrantly in the present moment, when

*you are connected to God and know yourself and God as
one, when you step outside your intellect, your mind, your
emotions, and your ego. Inside your ego structure, you
can be excited, motivated, and even driven, but that is not
inspiration. Inspiration comes from the invisible world,
bringing spirit into matter. You just have to reach up and
pull it down.*

That, in the end, is what Debbie will always be known
for: her willingness, her ability, and her passion for "pulling
down" God's grace from the ethers of spirit into the regions of
the earth. She never seemed to forget those still vulnerable to
the same machinations of the ego mind that had done so much
damage in her own life. It was Debbie's compassion for the pain
of others that drew so many of us to her, and it is the special
spark that permeates her work.

There is no greater demonstration of a power greater than
the world than that this book exists, through which Debbie can
teach and testify even now. Her sister Arielle does more than
keep her memory alive: she keeps alive the thought that Debbie
is living still, in the Mind of God, in an eternal dimension by
whatever name we call it. Debbie called it holiness, and she lived
the light of her holiness beautifully. She was a woman, with all
the wonderful, gutsy, human dimensions that go along with
that. But as she points out so poignantly throughout this book,
holiness was the higher, most essential truth of who all of us are.
Through her holiness, and through this book, she remains with
us now and will be with us forever.

MARIANNE WILLIAMSON

You Are Drenched in Holiness

Drenched in Holiness

Dear God, Spirit, Divine Mother,

On this day I ask you to grant this request:

May I know who I am and what I am, every moment of every day;

May I be a catalyst for light and love

And bring inspiration to those whose eyes I meet;

May I have the strength to stand tall in the face of conflict

And the courage to speak my voice, even when I'm scared;

May I have the humility to follow my heart

And the passion to live my soul's desires;

May I seek to know the highest truth

And dismiss the gravitational pull of my lower self;

May I embrace and love the totality of myself—

My darkness as well as my light;

May I be brave enough to hear my heart,

To let it soften so that I may gracefully choose faith over fear.

Today is my day to surrender anything that stands between

The sacredness of my humanity and my divinity.

May I be drenched in my holiness
And engulfed by your love.
May all else melt away.
And so it is, and it is so,
Amen.

I was in my fourth drug treatment center, and it was day ten of a twenty-eight-day program. For over fifteen years I had suffered drug addiction and the underlying insecurities and self-loathing that had birthed it. I had been in and out of treatment centers and could never seem to make it all the way through the program. At around the ten-day mark I would begin to feel strong, willful, and hopeful, and convinced that I "had it." I don't know what I thought I had, but the ache that had led me into the treatment center would usually fade away by this point, replaced by a desperate need to escape. But on this particular day, I was keenly aware of where my "prison break" would take me. It was no mystery, because it had happened so many times before. I would finagle my way out of the treatment center, claiming I was healed and had found enlightenment and freedom from my addictions. And then, either hours or days later, I would be back in the same vicious cycle of filling my small body with drugs, chasing a feel-good moment, and sinking back down into the depths of hell and hopelessness.

This particular morning, by the grace of God, I was finally able to see where the path of running away would lead me. And I knew, without a shadow of a doubt, that I couldn't do it one more time. I knew that if I ran away, I would either find myself back in the same place or, worse, not survive. Even with this awareness, the urge to escape continued to well up inside me, and the voices in my head grew louder and louder: *Run, Debbie, run! Get out of here! You're not one of them. You don't need this. You can do it alone!* For hours I turned my attention to this inner voice and listened. I wanted to believe it. I wanted it to be the truth. But the harsh reality was, this voice had let me down many times before. So for the first time I decided to resist the urgings of this voice, and I chose to at least explore the possibility that there was some force inside me that could give me relief, that could help me where I clearly was not able to help myself.

So I excused myself from my group therapy session (joyfully so) and proceeded down the dark, dingy corridor that led to the bathroom. I have to tell you, the bathroom of this treatment center was a disgusting place. It smelled like dried urine. The stench was almost more than I could bear. The tiled floor and the grout between the tiles, which probably had started out gray, were now black with mold. I am a bit of a clean freak, and my top priority is beauty. I need it. I crave it. This bathroom was neither clean nor beautiful. But I was so filled with toxic emotions and so desperate for help, I decided to do the unthinkable: I got down on the floor on my hands and knees in a prayer position and began to pray. I asked God—or my higher power, as they call it in the twelve-step program—to come to me, to help me, to rescue me from my pain and my self-destruction. My body was shaking, and tears were rolling down my cheeks. I was desperate. Although I had heard people talk about God in many twelve-step meetings, for me God was nothing more than a concept in my mind. The actual experience or knowing of God did not exist inside me.

For a few minutes I listened to the ranting in my head about how stupid this was, how disgusted I was to be here, and how embarrassed I felt begging some power I didn't even believe in to help me. I felt angry at God, at my parents, and at all those who had hurt me, believing that if it wasn't for all of them I wouldn't be here, stooping to an all-time low. I tried to convince myself that I could get up and leave, but my fear that I would die if I ran away now urged me to stay.

I thought back to the day before I had entered this round of treatment. I had been living in an apartment at Turnberry Isle Yacht and Racquet Club in South Florida. I owned a thriving clothing store in the Aventura Mall with one of the most prestigious men in the state as my business partner. From the outside, it looked like I had it all: I drove around in my white convertible Porsche, wore the hippest clothes, hung out with the coolest people, and regularly partied among Miami's nightlife until the wee hours of the morning. Certainly my outer shell looked just right. I was the girl who had money, success, opportunities, friendships, and the world at my fingertips. But in the quietness of my inner world, I hated myself. I hated my life. I was angry, judgmental, confused, and disorganized. I was tired, desperate, and lonely, and the only thing that ever took away my pain was the carefully selected mixture of drugs that I faithfully consumed each day.

The truth was that the drugs had stopped working long ago. And although I could barely endure the thought of having to live without them, I knew I wouldn't live much longer with them. Just two weeks before, I had scored a bottle of Percodans from a girl I had befriended who worked in a pharmacy. I thought I had struck gold when I met her. She was the answer to my dreams and the solution to the countless hours I spent trying to round up enough drugs to get me through each week. But on this dark day, this day of reckoning, that bottle was now empty. It wasn't that I had never experienced an empty bottle before, but there had been a thousand pills in this big brown-glass pharmaceutical bottle, and less than fourteen days later they were all gone. I now needed to take at least ten Percodans to catch a feel-good moment, when a few years earlier I had needed only one. The bag of cocaine I dipped the ends of my cigarettes into, to accompany my Percodan high, was empty as well.

Here I was, face-to-face with an out-of-control, all-consuming drug addiction, surrounded by ashtrays, empty cartons of Salems, and the bottle of 10-milligram Valiums I used to begin each day. I was obsessed with trying to figure out how my life had come to this. I seemed to be a genius at rationalizing, denying, lying, and making up excuses for my bad behavior, but on this day, with the empty Percodan bottle in hand, I knew in the depth of my soul that I just couldn't go on living like this. I couldn't pretend that I was okay for one more day.

All my clothes were thrown all over my room since I had ransacked every drawer looking for pills I might have hidden and dollar bills that might still contain a residue of cocaine. My purses were scattered across my closet floor from my tireless search, knowing there must be something, some residue, somewhere. All the plastic pill bottles in my bathroom, where I would typically hide a few pills here and there, now lay uncapped on the marble countertop.

As I had frantically searched, I felt the desperation, the fear, the powerlessness of needing a fix and being unable to find one. I could have picked up the phone, but I was too ashamed and humiliated to call even my drug dealers. No one could consume this amount of drugs in such a short time. No cute leather dress or outrageous dangling earrings could hide the pathetic nature of this scene. Even my drug dealers would know what a loser I was. When I realized that I would be embarrassed in front of people I considered the scum of the earth, I knew there was no other option. I had to get help. The thought that I was going to die had been second to the sleazy feeling of being a blown out drug addict—the poor little rich girl. There I had been, with everything, and yet with nothing, because I had lost myself.

After recalling this desperate and painful scene, my mind snapped back to the present moment, and I once again became aware of the cold tile underneath me. On my hands and knees, not knowing what else to do, I recited the Serenity Prayer: "God grant me the serenity to accept the things I cannot change, the courage to change the things I can, and the wisdom to know the difference." I focused intently on each phrase because I ached for some serenity. More than anything in the world, I wanted a few minutes of peace inside my noisy mind. I whispered the words, just loud enough so I could hear them, over and over and over again: "God, give me the courage to change." I wanted to change. I needed to change so badly. I began begging and crying hysterically. With my head in my hands, I sobbed uncontrollably until I suddenly realized that something inside me had shifted. A calm had come over me—a silence that was palpable. In asking God, this higher power, to enter my awareness, something inside me had opened up and relaxed. The stress in my body had released, and the screaming voice in my mind had subsided. Peace had enveloped my entire self. Even the filthy, disgusting bathroom floor didn't look so bad. There was a release inside me, a letting go, a clarity, an expansiveness, but more importantly, there was hope. My God, I had hope. Just what I needed.

That morning I had experienced something very special. Even though I didn't know what it was, it had lifted me out of the pain of my emotional body, at least for the time being, and brought me to the perfection of the present moment. I knew then that I could make it through another day. And at that point, one more day was all I really needed. Suddenly I was filled with joy and excitement, and I wanted to stand up and shout out to the world, "I can do it!"

I share with you this experience on the bathroom floor of the Palm Beach Institute because it was the moment when

I knew that a power greater than myself existed. It was the moment when I began to heal and transform my inner world and form a deep, loving relationship with the power that I now know as God. Every day for the next eighteen days, I made the choice to find my way back into that bathroom, which became my holy sanctuary—a place where I could reconnect with the all-loving presence that had delivered me to a higher aspect of myself. Through this daily ritual I found the strength to finally make it through all twenty-eight days of treatment.

On a warm summer day nearly twenty-four years ago, I walked out of my last treatment center, knowing that I had tapped into a power and a source that could move mountains, change people's lives, and lead me to a future that I couldn't even fathom yet. I knew in every cell of my being that I needed to further explore, understand, and devote myself to finding and knowing God. Hallelujah!

> Dear God,
> Dance with me.
> Hold me tight like a lover.
> Spin me around until a smile covers my face.
> Lift me up, and when my feet touch the ground,
> Let me know that I am one with you.

As I resumed my life, I was consumed by the need to understand how this shift had occurred. Why had I found the strength this time that I had failed to find so many times before? How had I gone from feeling deep pain, agony, and despair to experiencing peace, joy, and contentment? How had I felt so alone and separate one moment, then, a moment later, completely connected, one with all that is, seen and unseen?

How had I gone from seeing the world through the self-centered eyes of my wounded ego to glimpsing the unbelievable intricacies of my spiritual path?

To this day I remain awed and fascinated by what's available to any one of us when we open ourselves up to the unseen forces that exist within and around us. The quest to understand this powerful source has led me on a long, unbelievable journey, from the depths of darkness and despair to unimaginable moments of light, love, creativity, and joy. And now, excitedly, I share with you what I have learned from the greatest spiritual teachers of our time, as well as the ancient sages and spiritual masters whose teachings continue to live on in our awareness. In the pages that follow, you will find a process that will unleash this power within you, so that you can heal your heart at the deepest level and return to your rightful nature, your truest essence . . . your holiness.

The Shift

Dear God,
Open me up so that I may know you.
Show me your sweetness in the smiles I see.
Open me up to the love that you are
While you awaken me to the love that I am.

What happened on the bathroom floor that day, I now know, is what's called a "shift in consciousness." For a few moments I was lifted out of the pain of my emotional body and the insanity of my tumultuous mind, and transported to a place that is all loving, all knowing, quiet, secure, and relaxed. I had entered the "holy land," where God consciousness resides. In just a few moments— and that's all it took—I was able to open a place inside myself that had the power to shift and change my entire life.

This shift is available to any of us at any time because it requires nothing more than for us to slip out of our separate human experience and reconnect with the part within us that is one with the divine source. Ask and we shall receive. Our willingness to ask is what opens the door. Our willingness to admit that we do not know everything, and that the smallness of our individual selves means they are not able to do it all on their own, unhooks us from the trance of our individual realities. Once we are able to own up to this truth and concede that we can't do this alone, the lower aspects of us settle down and the door to the higher realms opens. This is what allows for the shift to occur. The divine does not push us or invite itself through the closed door of our lower selves. It respectfully allows us to make the choice to live an ego-driven life or a God-centered life. In other words, we can choose to take the difficult road of doing it our way, on our own, or to surrender to a higher will, God's will, and live in partnership with the greater whole. If we choose the latter, we must ask that our hearts remain open and extend the invitation to which God will gracefully respond by reentering our awareness. When divine consciousness enters, the shift occurs and we are engulfed by the love of our higher selves.

We make the space inside, for God to enter, by opening up to a larger reality than the one we are presently living in. When the divine enters, we can feel it. It shifts our thoughts, which shifts our feelings. Emmet Fox, a man I believe is one of the greatest spiritual leaders of the twentieth century, tells us, "This state of mind is really the one thing that is worth possessing, for having that, one has all; and lacking that, one has nothing." To reach this state is the real object of prayer. He goes on to say that prayer truly does deliver us to a "'holy' place, because nothing defiled in any way can reach us there." In this higher state of consciousness we know we are protected, powerful, and strong. We know we have the power to make trauma, heartache, dis-ease, negative emotions, and other day-to-day problems of life disappear. That's right, disappear. When we are one with our creator, when we are willing (pay attention to this word) to not know, to not understand, to not have it all figured out, to not be in charge, to not have life go the way we think it should go, then miracles can happen. Life can surprise us only when we are willing to be surprised. And what does that take? It takes living a God-centered life. It takes not knowing. This is the life-changing shift, to open up to new realities over and over and over again and to let go of the illusion that what we see and what we know is right or real.

Many of our beliefs and intellectual knowledge, while justified, are limited. They may be perfectly correct in the small confines of our emotional world or our intellectual understanding, but this is not what we are talking about here. In universal consciousness—God consciousness—most of what we consider to be facts about ourselves probably are not. What we know and what we are certain about are probably the limiting beliefs that keep the door closed to our higher selves and to divine consciousness. Each moment we get to choose to look through the small, limited eyes of our individual consciousness or to be humble enough to take the leap outside what we may believe or know to be true and trust that there is a world beyond what we are able to grasp at this moment, a power that hungers to guide us and support us—a power whose plan for us is so much greater than our own.

To experience the shift we must become humble. Humility opens the door and lights the way so we can crawl out of the dungeon of darkness and despair. Humility is the most difficult state for the ego, because our ego views needing something outside ourselves as a sign of weakness. Therefore, wanting the experience of humility, in and of itself, asserts that we know we need God's help in order to be whole and complete. This assertion is a humble act and opens the door to the higher states of consciousness. In my opinion, humility is the greatest spiritual asset any one of us could ask for, because it is the gateway to experiencing heaven on earth.

So I ask you now: Are you willing to have this experience, to be humble enough to let go of all the concepts in your mind that you've been attached to? Are you willing to give up what you know and what you believe? If you are, you might just find the answers to your prayers.

Knowing God

Let me know God's grace.

Let me see God's face.

Let me feel God's love.

Let me return to God's embrace.

The God that I speak of is not an all-powerful presence that lives outside us, but rather a universal force that resonates in the core of our being, connecting us to all that is and all that will be. It's an all-encompassing energy that is creative, powerful, and wise, and a force that is often referred to as "spirit," "love," "universal consciousness," "divine order," "nature," or as a particular spiritual master. It is known by many names, and many paths can lead us to reconnect with the God presence within us. To deepen our relationship with this universal force, which has the power to light us up like a Christmas tree, all we need is the humility to step outside the grandiosity of our limited self and express an honest, humble desire to know God.

To know God is to know ourselves in our highest and purest form. It is to glimpse the part of us that exists beyond our limitations, our stories, our doubts, our fears, and our critical mind. Even though this force is unseen, when we join with it, when our thoughts and beliefs and feelings are aligned with it, we can feel it. Yes, we can feel it—it's palpable. God is a very real vibration that exists. We can feel it pulsating through our body. We can feel it through the love in our heart and the satisfaction of our soul. It's free and yet it's the richest substance that any of us could hope to possess. When we tap into the God force within us, we feel like we're royalty, lavished in jewels. We want for nothing because we have everything. Our divine connection is as precious as a baby's breath. It's pure, it's easy, it's natural, and it's peaceful. It's like being bathed in God's grace. It's intoxicating. It allows us to breathe deeply, effortlessly, and everyone who comes near it can feel it. It is who we are at the deepest level. It is our holiness, pure and simple.

The process of knowing God does not take place in our mind, but in our heart. No matter what we may understand intellectually about God consciousness, our mind can't take us where our heart longs to go. Our intellectual knowledge of God often prevents us from having the very real experience of God, because intellectual knowledge alone limits the possibility of something greater. When we are in a state of knowing, inside our intellect, it limits what we can see, what we can do, what we can feel, and what we will experience. Prayer lifts us out of our mind (funny—"out of our mind"! When we're out of our mind, we're free, we're peaceful, and we're connected and ready to soar). Prayer lifts us beyond intellectual reasoning to the level of consciousness where we have a direct experience of God. When we are willing to journey beyond what we are certain we know, we surrender to what the Buddhists call "beginner's mind." Beginner's mind refers to the state of an innocent child—the state of wonder in which we lived before we developed rigid beliefs and righteous opinions about ourselves and the world around us. This is the state in which we are led easily and effortlessly to the next right action, the action that will reveal our highest desires. But in order to return to this place of innocence, we must first relinquish what we think we already know. We must be willing to venture outside our mind and open up to the enormity of who we are and what God is. It is here that we become open and malleable enough to make the journey into our heart, where we will return to our holiness.

Finding Faith

Take me to the holy land,
Lead me to new landscapes,
Deliver me to your kingdom,
So that I may see through new eyes.

As someone whose faith has been tested more than once, I am
a firm believer that we must take time out of our life each day
to nourish our faith. We can't take it for granted that we know
God. We can have faith one day and lose our faith the next. We
can have faith and then not even know that we've lost it. We
can be watching the news and see that a young child has been
molested and murdered, and unconsciously we can get angry at
God, cutting ourselves off from our divine connection and losing
our faith. There are things going on around us in the world every
minute of every day that would make any sane person question
whether there even is a God. The moments that we take to fall
still, to reclaim our faith, to affirm that there is a God we are
intimately connected to, are the most important moments of our
day. In these vital moments, we reconnect with our faith, and
faith is the spiritual sustenance of our life.

Faith is a friend by our side. When we allow it in, it acts
as the floor beneath our feet. When we have faith, we trust
that there is a power, an unseen force guiding us. Faith means

trusting in something beyond what we know. Having faith that we are part of a bigger whole melts away our separateness and leaves us bathed in the wisdom that we are never alone.

At each moment we have to ask ourselves "Where is my faith right now? Is my faith actually in my fears? Am I placing my faith in the idea that I'm unworthy and that I won't get what I want? Or am I placing my faith in the perfection of the universe? Do I have faith that I will be guided to the circumstances that will give me exactly what I need?" Most of us misplace our faith. We have more faith in our pain, our past, our negative beliefs, and our fears than we do in our innate right to be happy. While faith opens us up, fear shuts us down.

To find our faith we must give up control, let go of the way we think things should be, and surrender—wave the white flag of defeat. Prayer is the spiritual treatment that allows us to surrender our ego's need for control and to regain trust in the divine nature of the universe. Surrender in and of itself is an act of faith; it's a gift that we give ourselves. It's saying "Even though I feel scared or I'm not sure where I'm going, I trust that all will turn out in my highest and best interest." It is a sign that we have chosen to trust that a higher power will tend to our needs and guide us in the direction of our heart's truest desires—and this trust is the healing balm that restores our faith.

Divine faith offers us hope, possibility, and promise. It opens us up to the limitless opportunities that exist in God's superstore. If we choose to live in faith, we will be blessed with the support and partnership of the universal intelligence that is richly abundant in everything we could possibly need to live a fulfilled and blessed life.

Tuning In to God

You are there; I can see you.

You are there; I can feel you.

You are there; I'm coming home to you.

I love to pray. It makes me smile when I'm sad, gives me courage when I'm scared, and gives me a sense of connectedness when I'm lonely. Prayer is the holy process of turning inward, of coming face-to-face with our highest self. It is the invitation to enter, reconnect, and experience our holiness. Prayer is an ancient method of shifting our thoughts from the small self to the grander whole. It has the profound ability to raise our consciousness and heal our heart. When our heart is healed, it is naturally filled with hope, faith, and trust, and we radiate a confidence that affects every area of our life. Prayer enables us to rise above the mundane, transcend mood, let go of fears and anxieties, and reconnect with our highest self. Prayer is one of the few tools that support us in raising our awareness to a spiritual level, where our problems disappear. When we pray, we work toward only one goal, and that goal is to purify our mind. Through prayer, we rid ourselves of self-doubt and self-condemnation, we cleanse our subconscious mind, and we make room for peace, health, happiness, and hope. Prayer permeates our consciousness and fills it with divine love, which inspires us to soar to new heights.

Dear God,
Guide me,
Partner with me,
Hold me, and support me
As you lift me back up to where I belong.

Prayer allows us to experience the world through our most divine self and the blessings that exist all around us. When we look at our life and our experiences through the divine perspective, we see views that aren't available to us when we are looking only through the lens of our individual humanity. By accessing higher levels of consciousness, we open up to divine eyes that alter the way we see our life and the trials and tribulations of our everyday experiences. When we make the conscious choice to rise above our lower self, our fears, and our individual reality, we become privy to information, insights, and ideas that aren't available to us when we are looking through the narrow limits of our human perspective . . . our human eyes.

Prayer is the powerful tool that returns us to our most divine expression and opens the door to higher planes of consciousness. Prayer allows us to elevate ourselves, at any moment, from the gravitational pull of a stressful situation, whether it's a hurtful exchange with a loved one, a difficult circumstance at work, or a horrible act of violence taking place in the world. Through the vehicle of prayer, we are able to navigate our way out of the darkness of our heartache and negative feelings and find our way back into the loving embrace of our higher self. If we ask the universe to be our partner and guide us on the path to wholeness, it will oblige. As the Bible tells us, and as I will remind you often, "Ask and you shall receive."

The Matrix of Multiple Realities

I exist all at once.
I am everything I see.
Turning the kaleidoscope of my mind
Opens me to the magic of new realities.

Did you know that divine consciousness and human consciousness coexist and are operating within each one of us all the time? Right now a full range of experience and emotion is available to you as a human being. You can be burdened by fear, sadness, and suffering as you struggle against your perceived flaws and limitations. And the very next minute you can be filled with love, joy, and an exhilarating sense of freedom as you embrace the divine perspective and realize that you are much more than the sum of all your parts. The level of consciousness you choose to tune in to each moment of each day will determine the quality of your experience of the world. This is because everything in this universe carries a particular vibration. Everything in the universe is made up of electromagnetic energy that vibrates at different frequencies. Fear, resentment, and depression vibrate at a lower level than love, joy, and appreciation. When you're vibrating at a low level of consciousness, you see only what isn't working. You focus on the negative, on your weaknesses, shortcomings, and unfulfilled desires. And when you're vibrating at a high level of consciousness, the world and everyone in it is as it should be. You easily see possibilities and solutions; you are naturally in the flow, excited and passionate about your life. You're at peace with who you are.

So what's the problem?

If you're not living inside the state of consciousness that supports you in expressing your highest self, you will inevitably fall prey to the devilish vibrations of your lowest self. Like different websites on the Internet, every state of consciousness that you "click on," placing your thoughts or awareness on it, opens up different emotions, different experiences, and ultimately a different view of reality. This means at any time you can click on www.disappointment.com and dip into the feelings of disappointment you have about your life, your choices, or the bad behaviors of others toward you.

If that doesn't do it for you, you may want to pay a visit to www.resignation.com, where you are certain to find evidence that you will never change and your life will never get better. While surfing on the dark side of life, you are led to other dark states of consciousness. On the resignation website, you're likely to see a pop-up window—a great place for anger to advertise. The words are compelling—"Grudges welcome"—so you click on it. The site presents all the different variations of anger. There's a video clip of road rage in which you see someone driving fast and screaming, "You idiot! What are you thinking? Get off your cell phone and learn how to drive!" You can almost feel this person's blood pressure rising as he is taken over by an explosive rage. Something about this website is comforting. You take a deep exhale as suddenly you don't feel so bad about your own behavior.

Another site, www.anger.com, offers you the perfect opportunity to dwell on and justify your resentments—whether with the people you work with, with your circumstances at home, with yourself, or with the world. Frustration is here as well. "Don't forget about me," it irritably shouts out. "Why be angry, sad, or depressed when you could just be frustrated?" The vibration of frustration exists along with all the others in this moment, so it has quite a few emotions to compete with. And like any construct inside a healthy ego, it wants and needs attention. It likes to take over when life is not going your way or people are not doing what they said they would do or when you are caught up in a cycle of wishing and wanting something and getting nowhere. "For God's sake" is its mantra, and saying it invites the annoying feeling of frustration to fill you up and take you off the plane of consciousness where contentment and peace reside.

Of course your consciousness-surfing tour would not be complete without paying a visit to www.fear.com. Fear is a highly trafficked site that probably gets the most daily hits. It no longer has to advertise because its popularity is tremendous. Some would say it's as popular as Oprah. Fear knows that everyone can dip into it at any moment, and it seizes every opportunity to insert self-doubt into even the strongest minds. It likes to implant subtle doubts and erode feelings of certainty, and it gets off on watching how quickly a human being will sell his or her soul to visit it. *Be careful, watch out . . . Are you sure? People may not like you if you're too great . . . Maybe you don't really have what it takes . . . There are so many people smarter than you . . . You'll be all alone if you speak your truth. They won't love you if you open your mouth.* Fear of loss, fear of failure, fear of the unknown, and fear of rejection—all these emotions and the states of consciousness they carry with them coexist in this moment. Any and all these states are available to you right now.

Along with the low-level dot-coms, high-vibrational dot-coms are hanging out there in cyberspace: www.joy.com, www.happiness.com, www.peaceofmind.com, www.contentment.com, and www.passionateself-expression.com. All of these are available to you right now too. It's your click.

When we vibrate in harmony with our positive emotions, we take ourselves on an exhilarating trip "uptown," and when we give power to our lower, negative emotions, they take us on a depressing ride "downtown." This is where we, as humans, have a powerful choice to make. We can live in heaven or we can live in hell. Heaven is a perfect state of consciousness. It's the experience of being completely present to all that is and all that we are. It is the experience of embracing and abiding in the fullness of our human and divine nature. As spiritual masters have long said, both heaven and hell exist right now. People who are intoxicated with anger and hatred are in hell. People with incredible peace, generosity, and compassion are in heaven. We can pray every day and choose life-affirming behaviors that lift us up and carry us to higher planes of consciousness, or we can give up, be lazy, fall prey to the entitlement issues of our ego, and get swept away into the darkness of our lowest impulses.

If we are not committed to growing, evolving, and living our best life, we will inevitably search for and find an outer fix, some form of instant gratification to numb our pain and throw us back into a state of denial, so we can forget about what's possible for us. There we can try to stay comfortably numb, with our gifts hidden from us and the world. Instant gratification is always an option if we aren't ready to heal and return to our divine path, our true essence. Most of us have found ourselves off our path more than once, driven to make impulsive decisions that lead us away from our dreams and down a long, dark road to nowhere. If we do not take the time to care for our inner world, to nourish our holy self, we will be taken over by our automatic programming, which is usually inconsistent with our highest expression.

If you are reading this book, it is because surfing on the dark side is no longer acceptable to you. It is no longer an option, because either your pain is too great or your desire for having it all is too compelling. You want more, and you know you deserve more. You know there is something you're not getting, and you are ready to get it. Otherwise, you would be reading something else. So today is a perfect day to choose to give up control, take back the power from your lower self, and turn inward to God. It is there that you will have the will and the desire to bask in the peace, love, and joy of your heavenly self.

Opposing Forces

Let me stop the struggle,
Give up the fight,
Head down the road to freedom,
Return to the holy land of peace.

Two opposing forces exist within each one of us: the force that expands and uplifts us, that inspires us to share our unique gifts for the benefit of the world, and the force that holds us back, that traps us in the smallness of our lowest thoughts and feeds on our most primal, selfish urges. These two forces often wage an internal war, and the battleground is our consciousness.

I love the teaching story about an old Native American chief and his grandson. One day the old chief decided that the time had come to teach his favorite grandson about life, so with great presence he explained, "Son, there is a fight going on within the mind and heart of every human being who is alive today. Even though I am a wise old chief, the leader of our people, this same fight is going on inside me. It is as if there are two big wolves living inside me: one is white and one is black. The white wolf is good, kind, and does no harm. He lives in harmony with all that is around him and does not take offense when no offense was intended. The good wolf fights only when it is right to do so, and when he has to he does it in the right way. But the black wolf is very different. He is loud, angry, discontent, jealous, and bitter. The littlest thing will send him into a fit of rage. He fights everyone, all the time, for no reason. He cannot think clearly because his anger and hate are so great. It is helpless anger, for his anger will change nothing." The old chief stood in silence for a few minutes, letting the story of the two wolves penetrate his wise grandson's consciousness, and then he slowly bent down, looked deeply into his grandson's eyes, and confessed, "Sometimes it's hard to live with these two wolves inside me, for both of them fight hard to dominate my spirit."

Spellbound by his elder's account of this great internal battle, the boy pulled on his grandfather's breechcloth and anxiously asked, "Which one of the wolves wins, Grandfather?" Pulling with even more passion on his grandfather's clothes, the young boy asked again, "Which one wins, the white good wolf or the mean, bad black wolf? I must know now, Grandfather. Please tell me."

With a knowing smile, the chief placed his hand on his grandson's shoulder and in a strong, firm voice said, "The one I choose to feed, Grandson. The one I choose to feed."

This simple, poignant story reflects the plight of the human experience. Each of us is engaged in a continual struggle as the forces of light and dark battle for our attention and our allegiance. The light and the dark reside inside us at the same time, and we have to choose which part we will pay attention to and feed. Truth be told, there is a whole pack of wolves running around inside us—the loving wolf, the kindhearted wolf, the smart wolf, the sensitive wolf, the strong wolf, the selfless wolf, the creative wolf, and along with them are the dissatisfied wolf, the ungrateful wolf, the entitled wolf, the nasty wolf, the selfish wolf, and the destructive wolf. Each and every day we have the opportunity to acknowledge all these wolves, all these parts of us, and we get to choose which to focus on and feed.

Prayer is the spiritual food that helps us nourish and empower the good wolves. It's a must. It's one of the few things we can do to ensure that the good wolves win. It takes strength and courage to stand strong in the face of the dark wolves. We are deeply conditioned to fear them and give our power to them. That is why we need God. God consciousness will help us win this battle. God, Goddess, and all the other powers of goodness can do for us what we cannot do for ourselves.

At every moment—with every thought, word, and deed—we allow ourselves either to be guided by the God force within us or to be taken over by our darker impulses. We have the choice to summon the light or to remain susceptible to the darkness. Our internal darkness—our shadow self—is triggered in times of fear, loss, and rage, and if we are not diligent, we will get swept away in it, temporarily interrupting our connection with our spiritual source. The darkness that exists both inside and outside us is a force that must be understood and respected. It is a force that can bring us to our knees or be our greatest teacher. When dark impulses arise, a door is open for more darkness to enter. This is the universal law of attraction. It states that like attracts like. If we allow our darkest thoughts and emotions to flourish inside us, we add to our suffering and prolong our pain. Every time we are wounded, hurt, betrayed, or let down by either ourselves or others we must be aware that this heartache separates us from our divine source and opens us up for dark feelings to enter. When we are hurt, we are vulnerable. Just as after we have had the flu or an operation of some kind, we must take extra special care of ourselves. We must guard against other germs coming in and infecting us further. The same is true for our emotional wounds. In times of stress we have to be extra gentle with ourselves and diligent with our commitment to bring ourselves back into alignment with our divine source. We must fight hard and make our spiritual rituals a top priority. Without God, we will sink into a dark hole of the collective unconscious that is filled with more pain and self-pity than anyone deserves to bear.

While in the dark hole of your lowest self, the forces of evil or darkness eagerly fill your consciousness with self-doubt, negativity, and feelings of hopelessness. Do not let this happen, but if it does, work diligently with prayer and prayer treatments to get yourself out of it. (Prayer treatments are healing affirmations, where through prayer the focus of attention shifts entirely away from the problem and onto God's goodness.) Although you may have lost sight of it in the darkness, goodness is not that far away. It resides at the opposite side of the spectrum, but it is still on the spectrum.

The Dance Between the Inner and the Outer

With grace let me move between the inner and the outer.

With ease let me commingle with the realities that coexist.

Let my heart be open to the duality of all that I am and all that there is.

We're so trained and driven to look to the external world to get our needs met, to get the good feelings we seek. We think if only we get the right body or the right relationship, if only we get that project finished or have all the money we want . . . We're sure there must be something in the external world that will finally deliver us to bliss. It usually takes a cracking open of some part of our life—where we can't make sense of things, where we run into an obstacle that we can't control or manipulate—to return us to the holy place within that ultimately restores us. Events, circumstances, and experiences happening in the outer world will crack open the illusions we create inside our ego structure. I believe the cracks are there to turn us inward and to bridge the gap between the internal and the external so that we can return to our holiness.

I remember one of the many times when I gave up my prayer practice and allowed my extra-large ego to take control of my life. I was trying to reach enlightenment by depriving myself of everything and anything in the external world without nourishing or working on my internal world. At twenty-eight years old, I was lying on a beach at a club I frequented, sunning myself, off drugs, off alcohol, off cigarettes, off sugar, off bread, off men, off shopping, and off praying. I was empty and alone. Then this guy who had been pursuing me came by and asked me if I would go on a date with him. Without much thought, I replied, "Only if you put drugs in my food." I told him I didn't drink, I didn't do drugs, I didn't shop, I barely ate, and I no longer was having sex to make myself feel better, so if he would hide some drugs in my food I would go out with him. Sure enough, he did. I was devastated. After a few years of working so hard on my recovery, I had just blown it. I had given up everything for a quick fix that led me nowhere. After much anguish and sorrow, I once again understood that I had been trying to get in the outer world something that could only be gotten in the inner world.

When we are hungry for something to make us feel good about ourselves and we refuse to take care of our inner needs, we do stupid things. We repeat patterns that we know will lead us nowhere. We succumb to our addictions—whether compulsively surfing the Internet, shopping, viewing porn, eating, drinking, gambling, or smoking. Most people who suffer deep feelings of emptiness know there is nothing—and I mean nothing—that can fill that inner hole. The only fulfillment lies in reconnecting with a spiritual source. We must reach deep inside and nourish, massage, and care for our internal world.

Prayer is the answer. It soothes the soul, heals the heart, and tempers external urges. Prayer is the sacred process of opening up and reconnecting with our most awesome and inspired self. Without a profound connection with our internal world, we will never experience the true joys of the external world, because the two go hand and hand. Once we have tasted the sweetness of our internal world, we see that what happens in the outer world is not as important. Because we are present with something so much grander, so much greater, than we ever thought possible. Being divinely connected, living a prayer-filled life, ensures that we experience all the good feelings we long for without leaving the quietness of our inner sanctuary. When we are connected to our inner world, we experience what writer Franz Kafka so gorgeously expressed when he wrote, "You don't need to leave your room. Remain sitting at your table and listen. Don't even listen, simply wait. Don't even wait. Be quite still and solitary. The world will freely offer itself to you to be unmasked. It has no choice. It will roll in ecstasy at your feet."

The Hungry Ghost

I allow your love to fill the hunger of my
unmet needs.

May the hole in my heart heal today.

May the sweet nectar of your grace fill
my ever-loving soul

As I bask in the satisfaction of your
nourishing light.

Within each of us is a hungry ghost that is always craving more,
whether it's more money, fame, recognition, acknowledgment, or
material things. "Hungry ghost" is a Buddhist term that refers to
an aspect of the self that is emotionally bereft, starving to have its
needs met but not knowing how to accomplish it. No matter how
much we have, if we are deprived in the inner world, the hungry
ghost takes over, and we find it impossible to feed its insatiable
appetite. The hungry ghost is never satisfied. Ironically, though,
when we allow ourselves to bask in our connection to spirit,
we want for very little because we're so rich inside. If all we
ever prayed for, meditated on, and asked for opened up a deeper
connection to the divine, everything that vibrates on those higher
levels of consciousness, including abundance, would come to us.

But when we are disconnected from this source, we hunger
for anything that will give us the illusion that it makes us feel
better. The only satisfaction for the hungry ghost is to fill it with

God, with love, with higher consciousness, to connect to all that we are and all that there is. When we are connected to our true essence, we feel absolutely wonderful inside. That's how we know we are one with God. We're able to rise above the small, lonely feelings of our desperate heart, searching for their divine counterparts. When we're connected, we're able to bring into the world that which we seek. When we're filled up inside, we naturally generate love, compassion, and kindness for ourselves and for others.

Life truly is an amazing dance between the inner and the outer. We need the outer experience so that we will learn, grow, and evolve. But to go after the outer without tending to the inner, we end up empty and painfully disappointed. And to hang out just in the inner world—unless we have chosen the life of a monk or happen to be a saint—we likely experience isolation, loneliness, and lack as well.

When we are connected to our inner world, we already are what we seek. We already have what we long for, and most importantly, we know that we never have to create from a place of lack. When we return to our true source inside, we feel good about who we are and we feel worthy enough to experience the joy of manifesting what we desire in our outer life. When we are connected to our outer world, we see the kinds of experiences we want to have that will be fun, exciting, and creative, and that will support us in our evolution and growth, rather than desperately trying to attain something that will make us feel better in the moment. We no longer have to ask, "What can I do and what can I get to make myself feel better about me?" Instead, we understand the undeniable truth that we are whole and worthy, loved and lovable. We are able to plant the seeds of our desires in our well-fertilized consciousness and know they will come to fruition.

Prayer is the path that delivers us to our most divine selves. It washes us clean and tills the soil of our consciousness so that more life-affirming, holy thoughts and feelings can take root. When we are in the presence of our power, potential, beauty, worthiness, and light, we are not as vulnerable to critical thoughts of despair, self-doubt, greed, fear, blame, or darkness. When we are connected to our spiritual essence, we feel good enough, wanted, loved, confident, safe, and inspired. And when we are disconnected, we feel scared, small, weak, unworthy, unlovable, abandoned, and alone. As Emmet Fox said in *The Golden Key,* "If you are thinking about your difficulty, you are not thinking about God." Through the vehicle of prayer, we come to know God. Through the power of prayer, we come to know our holiness.

Opening Up

Release me from my past.
Unleash the limitations of my awareness.
Open me up so that I may hear you.
Return me to the arms of your grace.

Returning to our holiness requires us to open up, to admit that we don't know it all, and to surrender our will in order to be guided by forces that are larger than ourselves. What is called for here is a humble heart. The law of divine guidance that I wrote about in *Spiritual Divorce* tells us that God will do for us what we cannot do for ourselves. When we get out of our own way and let go of our defenses, we become humble. Humility is the doorway through which the divine can walk into our life. Without humility, we believe we can do it ourselves. Without humility, our false sense of pride, or ego, prohibits us from seeing the entire situation. It keeps us from seeing with clear eyes. The ego remains in charge until we step outside our righteous belief that we are independent, separate beings. As long as this myth is intact, we keep the door closed to higher wisdom. Humility allows us to surrender all that we know, all that we don't know, and all that we think we should know so that we can return to an open state, through which God can enter. This is what it takes.

For most humans, returning to a humble state is easier said than done. But this, too, we can pray for. We must pray to know our entire self, not just a part of our self. It is counterintuitive to what many teach, but to know oneself is most often to limit oneself. To the extent we cling to being right about who we are and to the "truth" of our life, our beliefs will blind us. We will be unable to see the full spectrum of what's possible when we embrace our divinity. Most of us would rather remain closed and cling tightly to our inadequacies and limitations than to journey beyond the boundaries of what our ego thinks is real. But in the words of author Elizabeth Appell, "And the day came when the risk to remain closed in a bud became more painful than the risk it took to blossom." This risk is a choice we must all make. When I am in need of assistance to get out of my own small, limited reality I use this moving quote as a prayer.

A Humble Heart

Dear God,

On this day I ask that you support me in stepping out of the confines of my ego and into your sacred arms.

I acknowledge today that there is only so much I can have or do on my own.

I admit that my greatness exists in being able to admit to my smallness.

I admit that I am not the greatest manager of my own life

And that you, God, and only you, have the power to return me to the holy land, the land of the most high.

So today I ask that you take me as your partner,

That you use me as you will,

That you guide me to live your highest vision of my life,

That you use me to serve and be of service.

My life is yours, and I thank you for bringing me in and making me your partner in perfection.

I feel you now by my side.

I feel the calm of knowing you are there.

I feel the soft sense of love flooding my entire being.

My humble heart thanks you and blesses you.
And so it is, and it is so,
Amen.

Your ego is designed to be right about what it knows, what it feels, and what it believes. It wants you to be right about all the things you believe about yourself, whether that is you're unworthy, you're not good enough, you're flawed, you can't do it, or you can't have it all. Your ego wants to be right about how your life is going to turn out, even if that means you have to screw up your life. When you are firmly rooted inside your ego structure, your connection to your higher power still exists, but the channel through which you can experience it becomes blocked by the confines of your ego, the constriction of your ego's grasp. I love the acronym for ego: Easing God Out. When you identify with the smallness of your individual ego, you separate yourself in consciousness from that universal presence that is God. This is a great paradox, because in life, to be a human being is to have an ego. You need your ego. It supports you in distinguishing yourself from others. But when you fail to recognize that your ego is just one part of who you are, you shut the door on God. You ease God out. The channel through which you experience God closes and you're trapped inside your ego's limited perspective. When you're inside your ego, you can think about God and talk about God, but you can't feel God, and it's not until you can feel God that you will truly know God. When you're connected to spirit, you bring conscious awareness, love, and compassion to your ego. This allows you to open up. The more divine light and love you give to yourself and your precious wounded ego, the deeper your connection will be to the divine. It is easy to make the ego wrong and label it the "black sheep" of the family. But it's not. Your ego plays a vital role. It just needs to be reminded that it plays only one role; it's just a part of who you are.

What often gets in the way for many of us who turn to God, a higher power, or a spiritual path is spiritual pride. We turn inward because the life we are living has led us astray. We may feel a void of meaning in our life and a hunger for fulfillment. We seek God with the hope that we will experience more love, more connection, and more satisfaction. We read voraciously to fill our mind with words and thoughts about God. We pray, meditate, dance, chant, and sing to get closer to our beloved, to know God, to have God change our inner world so that we may find peace. But here's the tricky part: we often fall into the trap of spiritual arrogance. When we don't acknowledge that we are human beings, ego-driven beings, when we don't have the proper structures or feedback systems in place, we unknowingly slip out of our divine connection and slip back into our now spiritually sophisticated ego. With all our new spiritual distinctions, the ego is now loaded with ammunition to protect itself and keep it alive. It now has new language to use and a new mask to hide behind. Remember, the ego in its grandest form wants to believe it is God, that there is no greater power, that it's bigger than life and bigger than everyone else. The ego prides itself on knowing more and being more than the other guy or gal, so it mercilessly and ruthlessly finds ways to disguise itself. So here we are, thinking we are beyond the ego, so good, so bright, so knowledgeable, so above the common unconscious family member or idiotic coworker. We assume, because our spiritually updated ego tells us, that our perception comes from our spiritual essence when, in truth, it is often just a newly evolved form of our ego's operating system, otherwise known as spiritual pride.

It becomes more complex to try to question ourselves and see ourselves clearly without activating the insecure, doubt-filled, scared ego, which believes we are really with God when in fact we have eased God out. Spiritual pride, unfortunately, is now rampant in our world, because there are so many people who know so much. We have had deep spiritual experiences. We have visited the higher realms of awareness. We have tasted connectedness. Because of this, we must be diligent. We must stay steadfast and humble, in full awareness that we cannot capture true spirituality, that we cannot lock ourselves into God consciousness. We must not take our connection for granted or forget that arrogance is the devil's trap door. This trap door threatens to cut us off from our divine essence.

I can tell you I have fallen through the trap door too many times myself. You might imagine that since I teach this I would be immune—at least that is what I used to believe—but I'm not. So many times I believed I was standing in my holiness, my divine essence, when in truth I was deeply rooted in my humanness. My sometimes-nasty little trickster of an ego disguised itself so well that until I hit a brick wall, I was unable to see that I had lost the one thing that had given me more than I ever believed possible: my divine connection, my commitment to being a living expression of God's will. It wasn't until I lost money, love, or my physical health that I was able to escape the strong hold of my ego's grip and return to the subtle grace of my spiritual essence.

> Relieve me of my arrogance,
>
> Relieve me of my pride,
>
> Relieve me of my know-it-all nature,
>
> And place me by your side.

This is the amazing lesson I learned: It's your job to enroll your ego in your mission to live a divinely inspired life. You must show the ego the benefits of joining forces with the holy aspects of yourself. You must assure your ego that you are not here to wipe it out but instead to support it in getting all its needs met. You must take charge of the grandness of your human experience and let your ego know that you will embrace it all—your humanity and your divinity.

Once you stop easing God out and allow divine consciousness to be your guide, you will be able to receive the many gifts that are waiting to be opened and enjoyed—gifts and extraordinary realities that might now seem unattainable. For most people, these gifts show up like miracles. Let me remind you that your ego probably doesn't like miracles because miracles are an expression of a greater reality, a reality beyond your limitations. Miracles are nothing more than occurrences outside the realm of what you believe to be possible. So for a miracle to happen (which inside your ego structure can only happen if you are willing to be wrong about what you know, which pisses the ego off more than anything), you must again give up your righteous positions and limiting beliefs and what you believe to be the truth of your life. Prayer will help you to do this. Prayer asks the ego to step aside and give up control so the unknown can show up. Prayer, in and of itself, is the invitation for forces seen and unseen to guide and support you and make it all happen for you. If you go out each day looking for miracles, you will find them. They are there, I promise.

So you might be thinking, *If this is true, why aren't I just looking for the miracles?* Well, this is both a simple and a difficult question to answer. If you bask in God's love and light, you are already living inside a miracle, so you don't want or need much of anything. When you look through God's eyes, all the miracles that you normally wouldn't distinguish as miracles are clearly visible. You see the amazing power and intricacies of the human body. You marvel at the way the brain functions. You're awed by the sunset, the clouds, the changing of seasons, sunlight, a growing plant, the laughter of a child. Inside God consciousness, life is much simpler, because an effortless flow beckons you only to love yourself, your neighbors, your community, and your world. This divine realm calls on you to deliver your gifts with joy and impeccability and asks you to open up to all of who you are so that others may know all of who they are.

Returning to your holiness is a process of giving up who you are, what you believe, and what you expect so you can discover the spirit in you that is indefinable, unlimited, and spectacular. And when you're in the presence of this spirit, you no longer have to try to be someone you're not. You won't have to try to be good enough, smart enough, thin enough, rich enough, funny enough, special enough, interesting enough, caring enough, or selfless enough. You just get to be whoever you authentically are in that moment. You won't want the light; you'll be the light. You'll no longer seek the beloved; you'll know that you are the beloved.

If you desire to return to your holiness, here are the questions you must ask yourself:

How do I get quiet enough to hear the crystal-clear voice of God?

How do I let go of what I know, what I don't know, what I want, and what I need right now to quiet my mind so completely that I can hear the soft whisper of my creator?

What will it take to open my mind and let the divine find her way into my awareness?

How do I slip into God's dressing room?

How can I dissolve my fears and concerns, at least for the moment, so that I can undress, slip off my barriers, and let the divine dress me in the clothes that she has laid out for me?

Who do I need to be to step into the highest clothes that I am meant to wear right here and right now?

In answering these questions, you will meet and merge with your most divine self—your holiness.

The Call to Prayer

The Call to Prayer

Every night when you sit to meditate, pray to God unceasingly.

Tear the silence with your longing.

Cry to God as you would cry to your mother or to your father:

> *"Where are You?*
> *You made me;*
> *You gave me intelligence to seek You.*
> *You are in the flowers, in the moon,*
> *and in the stars;*
> *Must You remain hidden?*
> *Come to me.*
> *You must!*
> *You must!"*

With all the concentration of your mind, with all the love of your heart, tear at the veils of silence again and again. As constant churning brings butter out of milk, churn the ether with the ladle of your devotion and it shall produce God.

—PARAMAHANSA YOGANANDA
from The Divine Romance

Every religion, tradition, culture, and creed practices some version of what is known as the Call to Prayer. Although I have prayed in many temples and churches around the world, one of the most moving experiences I had was hearing the Call to Prayer while visiting Istanbul, Turkey, several years ago. After checking into my hotel room and getting unpacked, I decided to lie down and take a short nap. I dozed off, thinking about all the adventures that awaited me over the next few days, leading a Shadow Process workshop in a foreign land, giving interviews, and enjoying dinners, shopping, and sightseeing. I was so excited but already feeling jet lagged. My tired body tossed and turned for a little bit while I struggled to get comfortable, then suddenly from outside my window I began to hear a beautiful chant. It was like nothing I had ever heard before. A man's deep voice chanted words I couldn't understand, but the resonance of the chant penetrated my consciousness and immediately soothed my soul. Hearing it, my body relaxed and my heart opened up to a deeper place within me. A smile crossed my face as my spirit ached to know what was beckoning me.

I later learned that this enchanting sound is known as the Islamic Call to Prayer. Five times each day—at dawn, at midday, in the middle of the afternoon, just after sunset, and again at nightfall—everyone is implored to stop, to "hasten to prayer," to take out their prayer rugs, and to commune with God. I fell in love with this dramatic beckoning to the divine. Even though I am Jewish, I wanted to be included. I wanted to call out to God, to hear the chants echo through the streets, to live in a culture that was proud to serve the divine. It was like I was living in a different reality where God was first, and it felt so good. It was one great big spiritual commitment. Suddenly I didn't need to sleep anymore, because knowing that so many were in the mosques praying made me feel a part of something greater, grander than my individual reality.

Across the globe and for all of known time, human beings have found a way to acknowledge the divine source of our lives. In fact, there are as many forms of prayer as there are interpretations of God. Christians bow their heads with hands pressed together at the heart. Muslims pray several times each day, often summoning divine forces out loud. Buddhists pray to the "ten directions." In Tibet, fluttering prayer flags are thought to spread harmony and good fortune through the wind. The Jewish tradition is rich with prayers, blessings, and rituals to sanctify nature, special events, and rites of passage. Native Americans perform ghost dances, pipe ceremonies, and ritualistic burnings of medicinal plants when praying for healing. In the Hindu and Vedic traditions of India and Tibet, prayers are recited while turning the 108 beads of a japa mala. Gospel singers reach to the heavens with their voices and their hands, passionately pulling down and bringing in the connection with the divine. From Ramadan to the Jewish High Holy Days to the fall equinox, we pay homage to the profound mystery that runs beneath the surface of our conscious awareness.

So each day you must do your own Call to Prayer. With reverence, bring your heart and soul, your intention and your desire, and summon the connection that your soul is longing for you to experience. It seems so hard in this very busy life to take a few minutes each and every day, four or five times a day, to pay a visit to your source. This is the source that nourishes and sustains you, which can and will, if you so desire, bring you a holy life. Thank God for everything you have and everything that you will be given. And then, with passion and humility, ask to be visited. This is how we find God: ask and you shall receive.

Under Your Wings

Please, God, visit me today.

Help me to make wise choices,

Choices that will empower me and free me.

Help me cut the cords of self-destruction.

I need you now by my side.

I need you to take care of me today and give me the courage to transcend my difficulty.

Dear, dear God, let me know you are there.

Give me a sign of encouragement so that I can regain my faith.

I promise, beginning today, I will bring my heart and my soul to you each day for nourishment and wisdom.

I promise to give up control of my life and hand the reins back over to you.

I surrender to your love and guidance.

Thank you for taking me back.

I feel the shift happening inside me.

The lightness of a connected heart is beginning to show itself.

Thank you.

Bless you.

I am with you, so I know you are with me.

And so it is, and it is so,

Amen.

Your call must be passionate; it must transcend any and all other thoughts or commitments. Your call should arise from deep in your heart, demanding that you be retuned and united with your holiest self—with your creator. Only you can choose to walk with God, to cuddle up with God, to feed God, to pamper God, to sleep with God. Only you have say whether or not you will fully awaken to God in this lifetime. You are in charge— yes, you! You have the magic wand in your hand, the fairy dust, to transform your inner and outer worlds, to choose God first. How lucky are you!

The Daily Ritual of Prayer

Let the light of God flow through my heart,
my mind, my body, and my soul.

Let me open up to all of God's love,

For when I am wrapped in her arms,

I am one with my beloved.

While I adore these special times of holy ritual, the truth is that every day can be a holy day. Every day we have the opportunity to open our eyes, reconnect with our source, and experience the magic of life. When we pray, we are drawn within to the quietness of our inner being. This is the sacred common ground that exists among all forms of prayer. It makes no difference whether we get down on our hands and knees, whether we lie down or sit in a meditative position. We need only the willingness to disengage our minds from their usual focus, to be still and seek solitude. I found a beautiful verse from an ancient Jewish text that reminds of this. It says, "How can you not take time to be in solitude, to be only with the divine, when most of the time you are alone and unique? In your mother's womb, you are alone and unique. When you sleep, the body is alone and unique and the soul is alone and unique. In the grave, the body is alone and unique. Also, the soul is unique in the Garden of Eden. Therefore, listen and always walk with the divine and do not separate yourself from him for a moment. For if you seek the divine, he will seek you too and will not leave you. How beautiful and pleasant his company is, for he is your divine father who acquired you, and he made you and established you."

Rejoining with this divine presence requires only that you step out of the busyness of your everyday life and claim a holy moment. When you're connected, you're not run by fear, worry, or pain. Instead, you're in the present, certain that everything is as it should be and that you are where you need to be. Divinely connected, you know that higher realities always exist and that, ultimately, things are going to get better. When you're connected, you know that no matter what life hands you, you are guided and protected.

When I am praying, I like to close my eyes and stand in the presence of my prayer like it already exists. For a few moments I concentrate on my breath, consciously choosing to bring my highest self into my awareness, and then I set the intention to have my prayer penetrate every cell in my being. I ask that my prayer be kindling for my soul. I ask that it light a fire in me that will have me passionately go after my faith. In the moments I spend connecting with the divine, I ask to be shown what's right about my life, to be open and receptive for good to enter, to know that it's coming even if I can't yet see it.

In *Power Through Constructive Thinking,* Emmet Fox, my spiritual mentor, talks about prayer as a spiritual treatment, an instrument that enables us to raise our consciousness. He uses the example of a stepladder, saying, "If we already had a realization, we should not be needing the help of the prayer; we do not need a stepladder to reach a height on which we are already placed. The ladder is employed in order to enable us to raise ourselves, step by step, to a height above the ground to which our muscles alone would never carry us; and so a good prayer is a stepladder upon which we may gradually climb from the low level of fear, doubt, and difficulty to the spiritual height where these things melt away in the Light of Truth." So the words from the Bible—"Be still and know that I am God"—are an acknowledgment that God's presence is inside and outside us. When we enter into a prayer treatment, we must constantly remind ourselves that God is our refuge. God is our strength. But we must get quiet enough, *still* enough, to hear the voice of God. "Be still and know that I am God" are such powerful words because there is no doubt in them. They are a complete affirmation that we *know* we can connect because we know God is there with us.

Think about it. Would you act differently if you knew you were blessed, if you knew God was watching over you and protecting you and waiting to be contacted by you? What boundaries would you feel empowered to set? What requests would you make? What doors would you allow yourself to open if you knew you were divinely held? Would you begin each day looking for the blessings? Would you keep your eyes open to new opportunities? If you knew there was an extraordinary design for your life that was just waiting to be revealed, would you give yourself a break from questioning, from not being sure, and from resignation and disappointment? I believe you would. If you knew without a doubt that there was a God who was indeed on your side, you would make a holy demand on yourself to live your faith rather than your fear, and be returned *now* to your true essence—your holiness.

The Powerful
Process of Prayer

Let me surrender my will and give up my agendas
so that I may go where you want to take me.

Let me be humble enough to know that you know
what is best for me.

Let me be trusting enough to believe that you
want the best for me.

Let me follow your lead, listening for the exact
steps that will direct me to a complete experience
of you.

Let me glide across the floor of this day with grace,
ease, and joy.

Prayer brings about the gradual expansion and unfolding of
our awareness. When we pray, we use our words, our will,
our heart, and our intention to go beyond our mind. We
recite sacred words to open up the channel through which we
experience God. But what does it take to let prayer in, to have
it resonate within us so that we become open and receptive
to achieving the essence of that which we are seeking? To
understand this, we must explore the precise steps that unfold
when we engage in the process of prayer.

It begins with the willingness to be opened, to let go of our resistance and righteous beliefs, in order to experience something new. Why do we ask to be opened? Because most of us are shut down, closed off, and unaware that we are keeping God out. Although our mind may argue to the contrary, our heart is closely guarded. Pains of the past act as a veil between our lower self and our higher states of consciousness. As we humbly acknowledge this truth, we let our holy spirit know that there is a higher place for us to open up to. This call to be opened is our first request to our higher self.

We then beckon God in whatever name or form we know her to be—a higher power, a light within, the forces of the earth or nature, or an ascended master—to be with us, to reveal herself to us, to infuse us with her power, love, and grace. We call forth this power, affirming that we are one with its presence, and we begin to feel it moving through our body, heart, and mind.

The next phase of the process of prayer is to clearly and boldly state what we desire. If it's relief from emotional pain, we identify and ask for what we want to feel in its place. If it's peace of mind in place of anxiety, we ask for peace. If we seek financial abundance, we ask for it. By clearly and specifically stating what it is we want, we are placing our order with the universe. The moment we admit that the experience we're now having is not what we desire, we open up inside and begin the magical process of calling in powers greater than ourselves to deliver us that which we clearly desire.

If we don't ask, we don't receive.

The next stage of our prayer's unfolding occurs when we generate within ourselves the experience of what we are seeking through our prayer. In this stage, we visualize ourselves already having what we seek. If we desire companionship, we visualize ourselves connecting intimately with friends and loved ones. If we desire abundance, we visualize money being drawn to us from unknown and unexpected sources. Doing this through our prayer, we claim our abundance, we feel our lovability. We know in every cell of our being that we are protected and cared for. We begin to vibrate at the level of consciousness where what we are asking for is already a reality. Thus, we answer our own prayer. We go from wanting it to being it.

My friend Gregg Braden wrote about this in his book *Secrets of the Lost Mode of Prayer*. He shares a beautiful story about how the Native Americans would pray for rain. They wouldn't say "God, bring us rain" or "We need rain"; rather, their prayer was to *become* the rain. They felt the rain on their skin. They tasted the rain on their lips. They felt their bodies being rained upon and imagined the ground becoming swollen with water. This is a dimension of prayer that Gregg calls the "lost mode," which most people are missing. It's the process of calling into being that which we desire to experience.

We have to generate the feeling of what it is we want right here and now. What does it take to transform from wanting something to being it? "Wanting" is thinking that something outside yourself has the power to give or deny you what you desire. "Being" is proclaiming deep within yourself that you already have what you need. You already have the resources to generate it, to manifest it, to allow it to unfold. This is the aspect of prayer that will radically alter your life, because to generate the inner experience that you already are and have what you seek, you most likely will have to move through the exact blocks within yourself that you will ultimately have to move through in the outer world. The moment you say the prayer, your fears will surface in your internal dialogue.

For example, you may want to be a powerful speaker, but you are scared to speak in public. You begin your prayer by saying, "I see that I can't do this on my own. I acknowledge my limitation." You then ask the divine creative powers inside and outside you—which are bigger than your every limitation—to come to you, to open you up, to give you support and help, to give you the courage to be that which you desire to be.

In the next part of your prayer you move into the realm of consciousness where you already are what you desire to be. You claim, "I am a powerful speaker." The fear that comes up when you step into that way of being in your inner world is the same fear you have to move through in order to manifest what you want in the outer world. Prayer gives you the ability to move through it right then. In a single moment, within the potent field of your consciousness, you can transform the limitations and internal conversations that have held you back in the outer world. When you pray, you come face-to-face with the limiting beliefs that have stopped you inside and gain the strength and perspective to rise above them. If you can't claim what you want in your private inner world, if you can't step into it and feel it as a reality in every fiber of your being, you won't be able to manifest what you want in the outer world.

The next part of prayer involves action. Someone once said that we have to "pray with our feet moving." Consider these questions, designed to help move you to action:

> *What could you do today that would move you toward the state of consciousness you desire?*
>
> *What would you need to say to yourself to raise your consciousness?*

What ritual could you do to seal in your new awareness?

What reminders or structures do you need to put into place to remember your intention?

It's been said that prayer without action is wishful thinking. Once we get into action, we step into the realties we seek rather than view them from afar.

A couple of years ago I lived in a house that had a spectacular view of the ocean. I would look out at the coastline, the ocean . . . the future . . . and I would ache. I wanted more. I didn't understand the ache, but I was hungry for something out there. It was so beautiful but so far away . . . so out of reach. Then I moved closer to the shore, and all of a sudden I understood what that ache was. The ache was now gone! It was satisfied because I was now living inside the view rather than looking at it from afar. I felt nourished and a part of what it was I had been longing for. And I realized that this is symbolic. When we look out at the future, toward something we really want— whether it's more money, a healthier body, a new job, a better relationship, or a creative project like writing a book—but we're only thinking about it, not taking dramatic action to be fully immersed in that which we desire, we're left with an ache. We can see a better future—something we want more of. That's the soul's signal: the ache. But when we take dramatic action and we move—whatever that move is, whether a physical move, a move to go back to school, a move to join Weight Watchers, a move to create a writing schedule and start to write a book, or a move to finish a résumé—that dramatic action shifts us from aching for what we want to already having the experience of it, the joy of it. We are praying with our feet moving. We are calling into action both the seen and the unseen forces of the universe, all of which are moving us in the direction of our heart's desire. This is freedom. The ache is gone. The suffering comes from non-action. As Mahatma Gandhi said, "Prayer is not an old woman's idle amusement. Properly understood and applied, it is the most potent instrument of action."

The next step is to affirm and proclaim that what we have asked for already exists on one plane of consciousness, or we wouldn't be desiring it. In that affirming, we choose to stand in the power and the possibility of the higher self, rather than in the fear and the doubt of the lower self. It's a beautiful distinction echoed by many spiritual teachers. "Be, then do, then have." In his book *Conversations with God,* Neale Donald Walsch says, "'Havingness' does not produce 'beingness,' but the other way around. First you 'be' the thing called 'happy' (or 'knowing,' or 'wise,' or 'compassionate,' or whatever), then you start 'doing' things from this place of beingness—and soon you discover that what you are doing winds up bringing you the things you've always wanted to 'have.'"

You first have to *be* it. Then you *do* it by taking actions consistent with who you want to be, and then you *have* what it is you desire. This is how the process of creation unfolds. So repeat after me: I know it. I feel it. I claim it. It is mine.

The final step in bringing closure to your prayer is speaking the ancient phrase, "And so it is, and it is so, Amen." I once read these profound words from an unknown source (believed to be written in the 1920s) about why we conclude our prayers in countless languages in this way: "When we have uttered all that we can utter, and our poor words seem like ripples on the bosom of the unspoken, somehow this familiar phrase gathers up all that is left—our yearnings, our deepest longings—and bears them aloft to the one who understands. In some strange way it seems to speak for us into the very ear of God the things for which words were never made."

Ending our prayers with "And so it is, and it is so" and "Amen" is an act of placing ourselves in the very hands of God, of trusting his will and his way. It is a reconciliation of our individual will with the will of the divine. When we say "Amen," we are saying "Yes, before God I agree with that. I believe that to be true, and I request the will of God be done."

Creating a Sacred Space for Prayer

How blessed I am to know you.

How lucky I am to have you.

How grateful I am to feel you.

How holy it is to be one with you.

Some cultures pray while in a sitting or kneeling position. Some bow their heads on a prayer rug. Some light candles, play music, burn incense, or ring bells to sanctify their space. Some like to gaze at images of ascended masters or other symbols of divinity. What's important is not the symbols themselves but the way they make you feel. You want to create a space for yourself that feels holy and allows you to honor and summon the higher realms of consciousness.

What kind of soothing, peaceful environment could you create that would invite you each day into the sacred ritual of prayer? What kind of sanctuary could you create in your home? A protected, quiet place where you can go on a daily basis to rekindle your relationship with the divine, a place reserved only for prayer? What type of environment most calls to you as a place to beckon God, to open up your heart and experience higher levels of consciousness? Your prayer space will set the tone for your spiritual experience. It can be simple or elaborate. You can make an altar anywhere in your home or office, with flowers, a picture, a candle, some incense, or a favorite prayer book. You can include in your prayer space objects of beauty, things with meaning, and images that melt your heart—a picture of a child, a lover, your best friend, or a spiritual teacher—anything that wakes up the vast wisdom within you.

Decide now what you want that space to look and feel like, and claim it as your sacred space where you will go each day to meet God and Goddess. Declare to yourself now that in this place you will think only nourishing thoughts—thoughts of love, peace, and loving-kindness toward yourself and others. Once you have found and created your sacred prayer place in the outer world, see the next chapter to create an internal prayer seat inside yourself—a seat of wisdom, where you are safe, connected, at peace, and able to tune in to the messages of the divine.

A Process for Creating Your Internal Prayer Space

Let me return inside

To dwell in the land of the most high.

Let stillness be my guide

And openness my path

As I surrender to the safety of my inner world.

Close your eyes, take a slow, deep breath, and put your awareness around your heart. Give yourself permission to see, to hear, to know whatever it is you need to heal your heart, quiet your mind, and open up the next deeper connection to God. Exhale slowly and allow yourself to float down, using your breath to quiet your mind and soothe your soul. Imagine that each exhale is taking you deeper and deeper inside yourself, to that very quiet place beyond your mind, beyond your ego, where you're connected to all that is. Imagine that you're floating into a beautiful garden, or any place that takes you away from your everyday life. Maybe it's a forest or a mountaintop or a beach. It's the perfect environment for you to practice raising your consciousness and opening up to all of God's love, light, strength, courage, wisdom, and beauty. When you can see your beautiful inner prayer place, imagine a prayer seat is there, a place where you can go each and every day to give yourself a prayer treatment, to raise your consciousness, to experience a holy moment. What does this internal holy seat of wisdom look like? Allow yourself to see what you would look like sitting in that prayer seat, knowing that this is your holy place. How does it feel to be there? What feelings embody, surround, and pour forth from you while you're in this space? Take another deep breath, then exhale out anything in the way between you and inner peace.

Now call in whomever or whatever forces you want present with you in your sacred inner prayer space. You might bring forth an image of Jesus or Buddha or a Hindu goddess, or you might call forth special guides, ancestors, or souls that you've lost in this lifetime who give you comfort and inspiration. Just ask yourself, "Who can support me in this sacred and holy time?" Allow these helpful beings to enter, and see them all getting comfortable inside your sacred environment. Allow yourself to see them gazing at you, nodding with encouragement. And breathe in that this is your time to know God, to know God as yourself.

Then, if you so desire, recite the next chapter's prayer out loud.

Feel Me, Touch Me,
Bless Me, Heal Me

Dear Divine Mother, Holy Father, God, Goddess, Creator of the Universe, and all my guides and helpers,

Bless me on this day to make this moment holy.

Bring forth in me the light of God so that I may know myself in the deepest way, in every way.

Help me to open my heart.

Help me to drop my barriers.

Give me the courage to stand naked in the presence of truth without resistance.

Let me stand in the divine knowing that there is nobody more worthy than me, there is nobody better than me, there is nobody less than me.

Let me know that I am a child of God, a child of you, a child of this magnificent universe, and let me know right now that I have a right to be here and that it's okay for me to claim my space, my peace, myself, and my relationship with you.

Let all those who guide me support me in peeling away whatever it is that keeps me blind to what's possible, that keeps me hidden from my greatness, that keeps me separate from my loved ones.

Today I ask you to lighten my heart, to lift my burdens, my worries, my fears, my anxieties, my grief.

Take them from me, please, right now, in this moment, so that I may cherish all that I am, all that you are, so that I may know a higher level of love and compassion, forgiveness and wisdom.

Let me forgive completely.

Let me love completely.

Let me experience my totality right now.

I thank you, God, for giving me the capacity for wholeness.

I thank you, God, for the tingling in my body that lets me know you are here.

I thank you, God, for this very precious moment when I am present to all the goodness that exists, inside me and outside me.

I see it now, I feel it now, I acknowledge it right now.

I know you are giving me everything I could possibly want, and I humbly receive your offerings.

And together with you, I say, "And so it is, and it is so."

Amen.

The Holy Cleanse

The 24-Hour Consciousness Cleanse

Dear God, Goddess, and any and all powers of goodness,

Allow the sweet sound of a quiet mind to soothe my aching heart.

Allow any dis-ease in my body or darkness in my thoughts

To spontaneously transform into nectar for my soul.

Allow my anger, sadness, discontent, vanity, envy, jealousy, and grief

To dissolve instantly and rebirth as spiritual nourishment.

Allow the force of my intention to permeate my experience

And reflect back to me the sweet nature of my deeper heart.

Let the voice of the divine return me to my holiness.

Today I choose to shower myself with your grace and your blessings.

Today I choose to reclaim my holiness

And be an inspiring expression of you.

You are my beloved, and my beloved is me.
And together with you, I say, "And so it is, and it is so."
Amen.

The process of emotional healing requires us to tend the field of our consciousness like we would a garden. We first have to clear out the weeds—the negative thinking and the turbulent emotions that we have allowed to take root. Prayer helps us do this. Prayer transforms our awareness—once clouded with judgments, self-criticism, and regret—into a quiet, tranquil place that perfectly reflects the mind of God. Once we fertilize the potent soil of our inner world with prayer, we are then ready to reseed our consciousness with holy and healthy thoughts, feelings, and impulses. When our heart is quiet and pure, it becomes a fertile field for God consciousness to blossom.

A Consciousness Cleanse is a way to purify and rejuvenate the soil of your inner world. It's vital that you take time out to weed and tend to the soil of your psyche, to clean it out, to stabilize it so it is fertile to grow new seeds—the seeds of your highest desires. A Consciousness Cleanse is a process of both letting go and taking in. You have probably allowed things into your awareness, into your consciousness, that are not of the highest vibration. These thoughts, feelings, and unhealed incidents grow like something toxic inside your awareness. A twenty-four-hour Consciousness Cleanse is your chance to clean these out!

To begin a Consciousness Cleanse, you must first acknowledge that you have allowed thoughts and feelings that are inconsistent with the vibration of love into the sacred environment of your mind, body, and heart. You must admit that you consciously and unconsciously, intentionally and unintentionally, opened up to these frequencies, and you chose to interpret some of your experiences in negative ways, which is what made them toxic to you. It's important to realize that your interpretations of your life's events are what make them nourishing or toxic. For example, if someone said you were stupid and you didn't believe them, their words wouldn't be toxic. The words would only become toxic if you took them personally and allowed them into your consciousness as truth. Aligning with the ranting of the internal dark force that resonates in the universe, listening to it inside your mind, letting in that lower frequency, builds up toxicity inside the field of your consciousness. Either you can beat yourself up about the toxicity of your darkest thoughts or you can decide today to cleanse it all out of your consciousness, body, and awareness. I highly recommend the latter.

During a twenty-four-hour Consciousness Cleanse, you make a commitment to refrain from putting anything into your system—your body, your mind, your heart—that is not of the highest spiritual vibration. To get started, declare a holy day: a day of prayer, reflection, refueling, nourishment; a day of Sabbath; a day to clear out the field of your consciousness. Set it up in advance with the people in your life so they know you are taking a holy day. Leave an outgoing message on your voice mail that you're unavailable to talk but people are welcome to leave you a message of love. Tell friends, family, and coworkers to deliver all their communications to you before midnight on the day before your cleanse.

Just so you are aware, your declaration to bring more spirit and godliness into your awareness may bring up within you everything that stands in the way of your highest connection. Werner Erhard, founder of Erhard Seminars Training (known as est), talked about how, when you call forth a particular state of being, everything unlike that state of being will come up. A Consciousness Cleanse will likely call up within you everything that is not holy, everything that is inconsistent with a pure and high vibration. This is just part of the process. You have to acknowledge that the toxicity is there before you can release it.

Imagine that for every negative thing that's ever been said or done to you, a little black toxic bead has entered your bloodstream. Allow yourself to reflect on all the years and all the people who have affected you in a negative way. All the people who said: "You didn't do that right." "You made a mistake." "You should be kinder." "You're so stupid." "No one will ever love you." "You can't do anything right." "You're just too needy." "You're a little overweight for my taste." "You're angry." "You're a selfish bitch." "All you ever do is think about yourself." Imagine all those words like little black beads in your awareness. How much toxicity do you think has built up inside your consciousness as a result of those words alone?

Now think about the things you have said to yourself, the thoughts about yourself that you've dwelled on, that you have believed to be true: "I'm not good enough, smart enough, educated enough, pretty enough, talented enough." "I'm not as good as . . ." Imagine all the damaging things you've said to yourself as more little black beads that entered your consciousness, blocking your connection to the fullness of your magnificence and your divinity. How many of these little black beads are there? How thick are they? What are they doing to your connection to spirit?

Think about all the behaviors, actions, and decisions you've beaten yourself up for—the things you believe you should or shouldn't have done, the things you've said, the choices you've made. Allow yourself to see the way you've punished yourself for these things over the years. Each of these incidents is again like a little black bead dropping into your consciousness, filling your body, your mind, and your sweet heart. How much toxicity has built up? What is the texture of it? Is it hard? Is it gooey? Is it light as a feather or is it heavy like sludge? Can you feel the burden of it?

Now that you are aware of this inner toxicity, imagine the mass of the black beads. In pounds, how much does it weigh? What is it like to be inside your body along with all the many toxic beads? Allow yourself to see how this toxicity has hurt you, how it has robbed you of your self-esteem, how it has eaten away at your confidence and your ability to love and be loved. How much energy has it drained from you? How has it blocked your creativity, your passion, your sensitivity, and your intuition? Mind-blowing, isn't it? Now take a slow, deep inhale and a long exhale, and let all of that go.

Beginning
Your Cleanse

Declare today as the day to cleanse your consciousness of all that stands in opposition to your true brilliance and the unlimited power of your holiest self. Give yourself permission today to allow all the darkness and heaviness of that toxicity to flow through you, to leave your heart, your mind, and your body.

You might want to find something—a symbol or a substance or a picture—that represents your internal toxicity and place it somewhere it will be visible to you throughout the day. Any time a thought or feeling arises within you that is lower than the highest thought you can imagine, say to it, "Excuse me, but you'll have to come back tomorrow. I'm not listening to toxic thoughts today." By doing this, you're learning to control your mind. You're demanding to be in charge of your level of consciousness. During the twenty-four hours of a Consciousness Cleanse, allow in only the voices of spirit, God, and your higher self. Tell any other voices that try to vie for your attention, "I appreciate you, but I won't listen to you today. I'll listen to you tomorrow." Or if you like, choose an affirming statement that lets your lower self know who's in charge. For the next twenty-four hours, anything that comes into your awareness that is not of the highest vibration, say to it out loud or in your mind,

"Toxicity, be gone. Darkness, be gone." Or simply place a DO NOT DISTURB sign on the door of your mind.

In the midst of this part of the cleanse, you can support your body, mind, and emotions in letting go of accumulated toxicity by using the cleansing powers of water and fire. You can do what I do after I lead the Shadow Process workshop, where a lot of long-held negative thought patterns are released, or after I've had an interaction that feels bad. Mix up a combination of Epsom salts and sesame oil, rub it together like a batter, and apply it all over your body in the shower. Envision it pulling the toxicity out of you. Put your head under the showerhead and imagine the water is washing away all the toxicity both inside and outside you, and carrying it down the drain. You can even say what it is you are letting go of out loud: "I'm releasing this hurt." "I'm releasing this guilt." "I'm letting go of this anger." "I'm letting go of this relationship." "I'm letting go of feeling bad about the mistakes I've made." "I'm releasing all the bad feelings I carry about the negative choices I've made for myself or others." Breathe in deeply as you feel all the toxicity dissolve. Imagine that an upsetting incident holds a particular color and see it draining out of your body. Envision a huge scrubber, bigger than your body, running over your skin, from the top of your head to your feet and ultimately down into the ground beneath you.

Another process that will support you in letting go and releasing negativity during your Consciousness Cleanse is to write down your negative thoughts on a piece of paper and burn the paper in a large metal bowl. I did this with one of the guests I worked with on the *Oprah* show. It's very powerful. As you watch your negative thoughts transform into ash, allow a transformation of your consciousness to happen inside you as well. Make it a holy and sacred process, letting the small flames in the bowl be symbolic of nature's ability to destroy and rebuild.

When you are done, thank God, the universe, and all the powers that be for taking away any residue of negativity from you.

You might want to do just a simple release by standing outside and closing your eyes. Take a slow, deep breath and look toward the sun while holding your arms out wide, beckoning the healing powers of the sun's rays to penetrate and mobilize all the toxicity inside you. Feel the sun beaming through you, its powerful rays melting away the toxicity as beads of sweat pour forth from your body and roll off you into the ground beneath your feet. Allow Mother Earth to absorb any and all toxic emotions and all negative thoughts and feelings. End this sacred process by thanking God for the powerful and healing rays of the sun, for supporting you in having the courage to let go, and for giving you the inspiration to change the things you can: your thoughts.

Detoxifying Movement

Dancing is another way to release pent-up emotions. There are cultures around the world that use dance as a way to connect with the divine energies, to raise their consciousness, and to leave behind the pain and sorrows of their past. When I lead the intensives for my advanced programs we use holy dance as one of the ways to release, to let go, to dissolve old beliefs, patterns, and negative emotions. We do a dark shadow dance where we all come dressed as an unhealed aspect of ourselves. We dance away our shame, our sadness, our grief, and our losses. We do a death dance to face and let go of the fears that we've carried around for years, the fears that have deprived us of our greatness, of our self-esteem, and of experiencing our holiness. We begin with music that stirs up the repressed feelings inside us, we call forth the experiences that have deeply wounded us, and then we just let our bodies go. They know exactly what to do. They know how to move, how to release, how to let go, and how to digest toxicity. You can do this at a Shadow Process or in the privacy of your own home. You can do it alone or gather a group of friends with the intention to cleanse your consciousness through sacred dance.

You might choose exercise as a way to release. Although it is not my favorite form of active release, because most of the time we do it for another reason altogether, if you make it your primary intention to release while you are walking, running, swimming, or hiking through nature, it will suffice. As you move your body to the point of sweating, envision anything you no longer need being released from your body. Stay present with the reason why you are exercising—to move toxic buildup out of your body and into the earth, where it will be absorbed and disposed of.

You can create your own way of releasing toxicity. There is no right way as long as your intention is clear: release, release, release. Stare into a candle flame, letting the light purify your body and mind; meditate on a holy person; sing songs of love and devotion; or chant the name of God. Any and all of these will support you in your Consciousness Cleanse.

Remember to breathe deeply during this holy day. Use your exhale to let go of anything you no longer need, anything that's not moving you forward, anything that is feeding your darkness instead of your light. Listen to quiet, soothing, uplifting music. Consciously declare out loud what you are choosing to let go of over and over and over again and what you are now willing to open up to. Declare now that the past is being washed away and a new future is unfolding.

Release Me

Dear God,

Sail away with me, my Lord, and let the winds
wipe away

My pain, my regrets, and my worry.

Let the ocean spray cleanse my consciousness.

Let the sun melt away the residue of my past.

Let the vastness of the open seas

Reveal the endless opportunities of my future.

Today I choose to make peace with the turbulent
seas beneath me.

Today I choose to lean into the direction of the storm.

Today I trust in the brilliance and magnificence

Of the One that created the great, vast sea.

Today I choose to feel the waters settling beneath me.

I am grateful for this.

Thank you, God.

The storm has died down.

The storm is now gone.

And so it is, and it is so,

Amen.

The point of the twenty-four-hour Consciousness Cleanse is this: either you're going to control your toxic thoughts or they will control you. This is the choice you must make. You have the opportunity when you're working with your mind to prove to yourself that you are the one who chooses the vibration that you live in. A Consciousness Cleanse will provide you with a much-needed opportunity to cancel out anything not in the frequency of love, compassion, goodness, kindness, openness, and possibility. Declare to yourself that you—yes, you—have the power to shut out anything that is inconsistent with these holy vibrations. With ease and effortlessness, you can tune in, invite, and open up to the higher realms. After your twenty-four-hour Consciousness Cleanse, you'll see the radiance of your spirit restored.

Once you've identified the darkness blocking your connection with your higher self, you can use the power of prayer to ask God to take it away from you, to relieve you of the bondage of your lower self, so that you are once again in the presence of your holiness. And for any and all darkness that you can't seem to put your finger on, you can pray that it too be dissolved. Choose a prayer to sustain you during your holy cleansing day. Ask yourself if you are willing, just for twenty-four hours, to let go of any negativity, any need for self-criticism and negative internal dialogue. Ask yourself for the willingness to take the next twenty-four hours to cleanse your consciousness, to re-fertilize your awareness, and to plant within the potent field of your awareness new, holy, fertile seeds. The prayer in the following chapter will help you dissolve mental and emotional toxicity.

Dissolve My Toxicity

Dear God, Goddess, and the universe, please come support me today.

Lift my ever-loving soul out of the dense fog of negativity.

Show me the sunshine of my life,

The fruit that I bear, and the gifts I have been given.

Let me open my eyes today to the light that I hold inside and the importance of my light in the lives of others.

Let me know God's grace like never before.

Lift me up to new heights so that I can stand on top of the mountain of possibilities and see beyond the limited perspectives of my current reality.

Allow me to see what will be available to me, to others, and to the world if I allow my toxicity to pass through me and dissolve.

Give me eyes big enough to see all the good that awaits me,

And give me the courage and the humility to know that all this good is God's plan for me.

Let me humbly accept this higher level of consciousness, where love and joy permeate my heart,

Where peace and serenity fill my mind.

Dissolve my punishing thoughts of shame, guilt, and regret.

Take from me any and all toxic thoughts and feelings.

I commit today to letting go of my stories of limitation, heartache, lack, and betrayal.

I commit to stepping out of the dark, angry thoughts of my broken heart.

I commit today to claiming the wisdom of my life experiences and using it to be a better human being.

Thank you, God, for always being there, even when I can't see you.

Thank you for coming to me through this prayer.

I am still enough in this moment to feel you enter through my consciousness.

I feel the shift happening inside me.

I feel your love, care, and understanding surrounding me.

My shoulders are relaxing as I let go of all my fear, worries, concerns, and toxicity.

For this moment, I choose to cleanse my mind and heart, and devote myself completely to you.

I am yours, and you are mine.

I thank you for this.

And so it is, and it is so,

Amen.

Encoding Your Consciousness

Let my mind send out signals that
convey my deepest desires.

Let the laws that govern the universe
work effortlessly for me.

Allow me the gift of encoding my
consciousness now

With pure love, joy, and goodness.

Having spent the better part of your cleansing day purifying
your consciousness of negative feelings and thoughts, you can
now begin the holy process of implanting new intentions and
encoding your consciousness with high vibration thoughts and
beliefs that will lift you up, inspire you, and light your internal
fire. Encoding your consciousness with godliness connects you
to the higher realms.

To encode your consciousness is to program your inner
world with fresh, holy, high vibration thoughts, beliefs, feelings,
and images. When you encode your consciousness with these
new thought forms, you embed within your mind and body a
particular vibrational frequency that resonates with the divine.
You purify the energetic signals that you are electronically

transmitting to the universe through your thoughts, words, and actions. With no toxic residue blocking your communication network, you send out pure, holy, high vibration thoughts and feelings to everyone and everything around you. Your intentions, now unobstructed by toxicity, are communicated secretly, invisibly, directly, and powerfully into the mind of God. What could be better than this?

The Ten Blessings
of Light

To begin this part of the process, imagine that for every toxic situation you've been in, for every negative criticism you have listened to—either from yourself or others—for every bit of fear, doubt, or despair you've dropped into your consciousness like a black bead, you must now drop in ten blessings of light to counter and uplift that negativity. Doing so will encode your consciousness with messages from the divine. In the same way cleansing your physical body of accumulated impurities allows you to better absorb the nutrients from the food you eat, cleansing your consciousness of toxic thoughts allows you to let in more nurturing, life-affirming thoughts and statements.

At the beginning of my career I worked closely with Deepak Chopra and David Simon, cofounder and medical director of the Chopra Center and author of *The Ten Commitments*. The Chopra Center offers programs to purify and rejuvenate the physical body, while my work focuses on the purification of the mind and emotions. One day after observing my work, David drew a parallel between these two types of purification. He said that many people come to the Chopra Center with their bags of supplements that different healers and doctors have recommended for them, and they wonder why none of them are working. He explained that putting nutrients into a toxic body is pointless. If the body is blocked by impurities, even the highest quality herbs and supplements can't penetrate the accumulated toxicity and won't be properly absorbed.

This is the same phenomenon that happens inside our minds. We can think affirming thoughts and read uplifting books all day long, but if we don't periodically detoxify our minds through a Consciousness Cleanse, new thoughts won't penetrate into our awareness—the mind will reject them. But once the mind is pure and quiet, once it is relieved of the turbulence of all our toxic thoughts, we open up the space, the welcoming and fertile ground, to encode our consciousness with higher frequencies.

So now I ask you: What powerful statements and blessings of light would you like running through your consciousness each and every day? If God were whispering in your ear, what would you like to hear? What do you think would inspire you, excite you, soothe you, and turn you on? What would God say to you? Allow yourself to open up to God's symphony. To hear the melody and the lyrics that will re-key you, that will solidify your connection to the higher realms. Allow yourself to hear the lyrics today, lyrics of love, hope, contentment, gratitude, and appreciation. Listen to the melody, the words, the silent peace that exists right inside your heart. Write them down. And then for three minutes every hour sit and plant these thoughts into your consciousness by reciting the prayer in the following chapter.

God's Lullaby

Thank you, God, for today is the day.

Today I open myself up to the music of the universe, the divine symphony that continuously plays when my heart and mind open up and become one with you.

Today I am in complete harmony.

I am ready to hear your lullaby, God. I am open to be soothed and comforted by the goodness that resonates within me and outside me.

Today I have the courage to listen to the songs of the heart and melodies of the mind, which are filled with love, hope, and endless kindness.

Your tunes, dear God, are soft, gentle, and inspiring.

Today I allow the music of the highest realms to dissolve any thoughts of limitation or deprivation.

I give you permission, God, to tune my level of consciousness so that I am in complete harmony with the divine.

I bless and thank you, dear God, for all the gifts you have given me, for all the gifts you have given others, and for inspiring me to harmonic perfection.

And together with you, I say, "And so it is, and it is so."

Amen.

You might want to make a recording of this prayer and include a few affirming statements that light you up and turn you on—statements like "I am so special," "I am cherished," "I deserve the best," "I create magic," "My life makes a difference," "My heart is filled with love," "The best is yet to come," or "I love myself exactly as I am."

Then you can play these statements for yourself throughout the day of your Consciousness Cleanse. Hearing the resonance of your own voice will encode your consciousness with all that you desire to hear, know, and feel. You can also write down these statements, put them up all over your home, and read them throughout the day. For twenty-four hours marinate yourself in your most loving, most positive self. Merge with your holiness. Enlist a loved one to call you and say the things you've written to yourself that your heart longs to hear. (And if you want to do this process with a buddy and can't find one, go to www.DebbieFord.com/YourHoliness and we'll match you up with someone.) Close your eyes and take time to focus on each of these statements, these affirmations of your holiness. Make sure you repeat each one out loud to yourself seven times, imagining the words entering you, breaking up the toxicity that has accumulated, and flooding all the toxic negative emotions out of you, onto the floor beneath your feet, being pulled into the fiery core of the earth and transmuted. Then, after the toxicity has been released, visually see these holy words being encoded into your consciousness so you can see them in your mind's eye. Breathe them in and affirm that this is your new reality.

This process is you telling the universe that you are ready and truly committed to transforming your inner world and reconnecting with your most magnificent self: your holiness.

Encode Me

Dear God,

I am open to receiving your brilliance and your light.

Rearrange my cells.

Let me think, speak, and act from my holiest self.

Let me be a vessel filled with you, my Lord.

I am yours.

Healing Your Whole Heart

Healing Your Holy Pain

Dear God,

Kiss me when I am sad,

Hug me when I am alone,

Comfort me when I am grieving,

Whisper sweet words in my ears when I need encouragement,

And cheer me on as I go after my dreams.

Life presents us with countless opportunities to awaken to our divine nature. Most often, the opportunities appear during times of great distress. It is during these times that we have the chance to explore our inner world and begin the holy process of becoming intimate with our entire self, our light as well as our darkness, our wins as well as our losses, our blessings as well as our disappointments. Pain allows us to break through the impenetrable walls and heavily guarded defenses that keep old habits, behaviors, and thought patterns intact. Pain pushes us past our limited thinking and opens us up to new thoughts, ideas, and realities. Pain forces us to question our behaviors, our choices, and our beliefs about life, and then to seek answers from places we've never looked before. It is our soul's way of opening the mind and heart to new ideas that will be the key to uncovering new realities—realities that support personal evolution, realities that will bring more joy, happiness, and contentment than we ever thought possible. Our pain, when digested and embraced, becomes our personal assistant, inspiring new beginnings and ultimately leading us to emotional freedom and reconnection with our holiest self.

A wisdom story has been passed down of a yoga master who once said that you will learn more in ten days of agony than in ten years of contentment. He explained that pain can be your greatest teacher—a friend telling you what parts of your life need attention, a spiritual wake-up call. He asked that you imagine being sound asleep when you are suddenly awakened by the fire alarm in your bedroom. Startled, you jump out of bed, run to the closet, and take out a baseball bat, smashing the alarm to pieces until it stops ringing. But then, instead of looking for the fire, you put the bat back in the closet, crawl back into bed, and go to sleep.

Pain is an alarm calling you to *wake up*. It's a warning, signaling to you that there is something that needs your attention—right now. It's a loud, internal noise telling you that an emotional fire rages close by, that something within you needs care and healing. If you want to keep open the channels through which God can enter, you must stay awake and tend to the flames that prevent you from basking in the gentler warmth of inner peace.

If we tend to our pain, we will be guided back to a place of peace and tranquility, of love and serenity. Pain is the sacred emotion that allows us to discover who we really are outside our ego structure. It leads us to places we would never go on our own.

I remember the moment when I realized my first marriage would not last, and despite the fact I had promised myself I would never get divorced, that reality was now inevitable. For some, the ending of a marriage may not seem catastrophic, but for me it was. This was in part because I had waited until I was thirty-eight years old, until I had found the perfect man with whom I could create the perfect life, and in part because I had promised myself that I would never do to my son what had been done to me. I had wanted him never to live with the pain of a broken family. But here I was faced with the devastating reality that my greatest fear would be realized and the end was near.

Although it took me many months of processing my deep emotional turmoil, as soon as I was willing to open up, to learn the lessons hidden within this painful circumstance, to see what life was calling on me to do and become, I got a message from the universe that quite literally made me who I am today. The message was that I was to heal my heart completely and then use the wisdom I had gained to contribute to others. The message was very specific. I needed to write a book called *Spiritual Divorce*. When I got quiet in my meditations and began to pray for understanding and relief, I saw that I was being asked to learn how to let go, how to forgive, and how to create two families who share one heart. Following this divine guidance led me to become a writer, a teacher, and a coach, to train other coaches, and to claim my destiny as a leader in emotional education around the world. If it weren't for the intensity of my pain, I would have continued on in the job I had been in. Six books later, I am still in the miraculous presence of what happens when we are willing to face and embrace our emotional pain. When we are willing to step into the storm and explore uncharted territories, we visit places we would never visit on our own. The moment we are able and willing to see the gifts of our pain, and extract the wisdom from our wounds, our pain becomes sacred and holy, and we are able to open up to previously unimaginable futures.

Our inner turmoil is meant to be a powerful catalyst to reconnect us with our divine nature—our holiness. Whether we like it or not, pain will propel us into a journey of self-discovery and urge us to learn how to love and accept the totality of who we are. Facing and deeply healing our emotional turmoil delivers us freedom from pain and prevents us from repeating the patterns of our past.

It's imperative that we use times of crisis and pain as opportunities to heal. Healing is the primary path returning us to a place where we see the perfection of our humanity and reunite with our holiness. It is this profound awareness that gives us the opportunity to return to the deepest connection available to any one of us: our connection with our divine creator.

The prayer that I used to recite daily, for over five years, down on my hands and knees, is a prayer I fell in love with from *The Big Book of Alcoholics Anonymous*. Known as the Third Step Prayer, it was my friend, my nanny, my lover, and my guide. It helped me separate from my pain while I was trying to understand the workings of my inner world. If you don't know it, spend a few minutes contemplating this timeless prayer, allowing yourself to grasp the implications of each verse, the meaning of each word.

God, I offer myself to Thee—

to build with me and do with me as Thou wilt.

Relieve me of the bondage of self, that I may better do Thy will.

Take away my difficulties, that victory over them may bear witness to those I would help of Thy Power, Thy Love, and Thy Way of life.

May I do Thy will always!

When we are relieved of the bondage of self, we are able to rise above our pain, lay down our internal weapons, and head down the path of freedom. When we use our heartache to help another, we are healed. This prayer is simple, to the point, potent, and life-changing. Use it and let your victories become someone else's lifeline.

Lift Me Up Where I Belong

Let the wings of the angels lift me out of my
earthly problems.

Let me feel the gentle embrace of divine skies.

Today I ask for the blessings of the higher realms.

I ask that just for this moment I know nothing
but the precious present.

I know with you by my side, Divine One, I can
get through anything.

I know that you would never give me anything
that I could not handle.

So I claim my right to pass through this dark time

With grace and ease.

I claim the power within me and outside me to
soothe my aching heart.

I choose now with the grace and beauty of a
soaring eagle

To hand over my heavy heart in exchange for
the lightness

Of a holy heart.

Thank you in advance for the love that I feel.

Thank you now for helping me lift my burden.

The Internal War

Let me lay down my arms.
Let me surrender my weapons.
Let my heart make room for all that I am.
Let the treaty begin.

The outer world, in all of its beauty and horror, is a mirror for each one of us. It is the macrocosmic reflection of our microcosmic interior life. Maybe you've noticed that there's a war going on inside? It's the age-old human conflict between our emotional, mental, and spiritual selves. It's the fallout of the ego's fear. It has us believe that we are divided, that we can separate from these seemingly conflicting aspects of ourselves. But this is exactly what causes a war in the first place. A separation inside us is the beginning of an internal war. It has us ignore the voice of our higher self, step over our God-given instincts, and violate our compassionate heart.

Are you internally at war with yourself? Are you giving attention to your inner terrorist? How do you wage war and attack yourself? Do you do it by attacking others, pushing people away, medicating yourself, numbing yourself, neglecting yourself, depriving yourself of the things that matter to you? Is it through demeaning internal dialogue or damaging and addictive behaviors? Do you make choices that leave you feeling unsafe and at risk in some area of your life? Are you embroiled in an abusive relationship or friendship? Are your dreams and future possibilities held hostage by a part of you that is stuck in the pain of the past?

It is the work of the spiritual heart warrior to tell us the truth and to shine a light on the darkness of our inner conflicts. We must bring love to these parts of ourselves we've separated from and ultimately reclaim them. To reconnect with our holiness, we must look at everything that stands between us and our God-given right to reclaim and stand unified with our magnificence. We will have internal conflict. It's a part of how we're wired as human beings. But each one of us has been given the divine responsibility to shed light and bring love to all of our selves: our holy self, our emotional self, and our intellectual self. That's what makes up a whole, the entirety of who we are, the holy enchilada.

There is only one antidote to the internal war that so many of us wage against ourselves before we even get out of bed in the morning, and that antidote is love. No, it's not just love; it's self-love. It includes making the decision to stop putting self-love off to some future date when we've finally become worthy. It's loving ourselves right where we are, and this is available only when we have made peace with ourselves for our perceived flaws, weaknesses, and sins. Here are the questions we can ask ourselves:

How can I love myself even when things aren't turning out my way?

How can I love myself even when I've made poor decisions and choices or when I haven't protected myself?

How can I love myself even when I'm fat and broke?

How can I love myself even when my wife has left me and

my kids aren't talking to me?

How can I love myself even when I feel flawed?

How can I love myself when I feel like I've missed my calling?

How can I love myself even when I'm scared to death?

How can you love yourself? You can love yourself by knowing that there is no other self. There is nothing else for you to do but truly love your inner self. That's what you were given. That's your job on the planet: to deeply love, respect, admire, and nourish your precious self, the spirit that only you hold. That is the antidote, the answer, and the solution out of which all good things will come.

For each of us, I believe it takes a shift in perception where we truly understand that there is no more time. It's not going to happen next week or next month or next year. We cannot wait for things to get better, because they won't get better while we're still beating ourselves up emotionally and psychologically and continuing to wage war against ourselves. And how can it get better if we surround ourselves with others who aren't in the presence of our greatness and are not willing to see the greatness in themselves?

We have to set a new standard for ourselves where loving-kindness, compassion, and acceptance replace judgment, ridicule, and rejection. We have to demand from ourselves a higher level of care, respect, and emotional integrity and then look for friends and a community that hold us there.

When we choose to lay down our internal arms and stop participating in self-induced war crimes, we begin to heal. So how do we stop the war? How do we lay down the weapons of negative self-talk, internal criticism, hating our bodies, wishing away our past, drowning ourselves in guilt, reprimanding ourselves with our regrets, beating ourselves up with self-destructive behaviors? There is only one way to begin. We begin by admitting defeat, accepting our powerlessness, and surrendering our right to use any of our internal weapons. In essence, we call a truce.

Surrendering to Powerlessness

God grant me the serenity
To accept the things I cannot change,
To change the things I can,
And the wisdom to know the difference.

When I finally surrendered completely and turned my life over to a power greater than myself, when I was able to feel the extent of my powerlessness, I was ready to let God enter my consciousness. I can tell you now that it was the sense of deep, deep powerlessness that led me to discover my highest life. It was my powerlessness that had me get down on my hands and knees. It wasn't until I knew that there was nothing at all left in the outer world that could save me. There wasn't a strategy, a manipulation, or a control that I could put in place that would help me. It was only when there were no options left and I had bottomed out that I allowed God to enter fully.

So today we realize how desperate we are to have control over our life, how much our ego wants to believe that if we assert our will or try hard enough, if we have enough plans or strategies in place, that somehow we'll be able to reach utopia—heaven on earth. And it's the cosmic paradox, because utopia can only come when we have completely surrendered, when our will is completely out of the way. When God's will and divine consciousness are flowing freely through our entire being, when we are one with God, we want for nothing else because our will and God's will are one and the same. So in order to heal our emotional wounds we have to get in touch with the powerlessness inside. All of us have experienced this as children, where we felt powerless or useless, where our environment was out of control. And it was then that our ego stepped in and decided that it would become the manager of the universe, at least our own small, personal universe.

So each day we have to take an inventory of what we are holding on to—what beliefs, thoughts, judgments, limitations, feelings, relationships, make us feel like we have some semblance of order, some power, some control over the future. It's only when we can make peace—complete peace—with our powerlessness that we can open the internal space through which the power of divine consciousness can enter. Since it is the child inside us that fights to control our day-to-day life, we must begin by doing a special prayer for that child inside, who feels vulnerable in its powerlessness. Most of us think it is ridiculous to take care of our inner child, or we refuse to acknowledge that this child is still alive and strong inside us. But if the child in us is gone, where did it disappear to? Where did the one-, two-, nine-, and twelve-year-old go?

Take a slow, deep breath and see if you can bring an image of the child within you into your awareness and then, gently and slowly, say the next healing prayer to her or him.

Sweet Child of Mine

Dear Child Inside,

I know how scary it is to let go, to release,

To feel the devastating effect of being powerless—

Powerless over your family, your friends, other kids who might have hurt you or teased you.

I understand how desperate you are to feel that you have some power over your life.

But today, dear child, I ask that you let go,

That you trust in a higher power,

That you surrender your feelings of powerlessness

To the collective divine power that orchestrates every move

In this complex and cosmic dance.

It's safe today for you to let go.

It's safe for you to acknowledge the devastation and heartache of the past that left you feeling out of control.

It's safe for you to turn your life over to the Divine Mother.

It's safe now to return to your holiness.

So take a deep breath, little one, and open up your heart so that your Divine Mother and Father can rescue you.

I see it happening.

I see your smiling face.

I feel your heart softening and your arms opening.

Thank you for this, dear child. I will take care of
you now.

After you have read this prayer to your inner child, take a few minutes, close your eyes, and see if you can comfort this part of yourself. You have the ability to re-parent yourself from the inside out and care for the parts of you that are unhealed and need your attention.

After you care for the tender and young parts of yourself, you can then come to this conversation about surrender as an adult, seeking guidance and safety in order to surrender your will.

Surrendering into Your Arms

Dear Divine Mother, Father, Creator of All,

Take me in your arms and let me know that it is safe for me to turn over my will to you.

My deepest desire is to align my will with your will.

I love you, God, for the patience you have had with me.

I thank you for allowing me to run around and pretend like I have control.

I thank you for the guidance you have given me and for allowing me to become the person I am today.

But today I admit that I have come as far as I can with my own will.

And I offer my life to you to be guided, to be supported, to be loved,

So that I may be the next grandest, greatest expression of your will.

In surrendering my powerlessness

I open the door to the greater powers that be, to use me and fill me up so that I may support others in filling themselves up.

So I accept your guidance and I accept your will for me.

I trust in your plan.

I joyously open up to the level of consciousness that will deliver me to you.

And so it is, and it is so,

Amen.

Healing Your Precious Heart

Transform my pain into wisdom,

My aching heart into fuel for my future.

Grant me the courage today

To treat myself like the precious commodity
that I am:

A million pounds of gold.

I see it all the time . . . We look everywhere in the world for love
except where we're actually going to find it. We try to find it in
our soul mate or partner, in our friends, in our bank accounts,
in our public image, in our successes, in our communities, but
it only exists in one place, inside us: in our holy heart. And our
heart requires so much more than most of us give it.

It needs gentle love and compassion, it needs forgiveness,
and it needs complete acceptance of its disappointments and
pain. Until we recognize this and commit to bringing the light
of awareness to ourselves, we have to continue our human rat
race of trying—trying harder, getting, collecting, wanting, and
hungering for more of something in the outer world.

Think about all the times you've taken your holy heart
and given it away, all the times you've put your holy heart in the

hands of people you didn't really know or trust. Think of all the times you left your holy heart at home alone, just so you could chase something you thought would make you feel better.

Imagine you had a precious baby you waited all your life to give birth to. Would you just hand the baby off to anybody on the street? Would you leave him or her for days, weeks, months, or years? Would you subject it to people who were spewing negativity, always pointing out what's wrong with it? No, you wouldn't. And you wouldn't do this to your heart either if you knew its sacredness. You would hold it, love it, and pay proper attention to it. You would worship it and bless it. You would be in awe of it. You would speak the most beautiful, prayerful words to your heart. The following prayer will support you in the process of healing your holy heart. Now is the time. So let's pray.

Heal My Tender Heart

Dear God,

Help me bathe myself in your love.

Help me know you even when I can't see you.

Help me open up to your magic and plant my feet firmly in the faith I need to grow and evolve.

Let your tender touch soothe my heart.

Let your encouraging words calm my mind.

Let your unwavering commitment to my greatest self comfort my soul.

My devoted bearer of light, I invite you, please, to visit me in my dreams,

Speak to me in my meditations,

Touch me through the gentle breeze and the sounds of nature.

Fill my heart now with the love that will end my suffering.

I know you are there for me, so I give you my thanks and gratitude.

Devoted Father, Mother, Carrier of Light, I surrender to you today.

And so it is, and it is so,

Amen.

Returning from Life's Heartaches

This too shall pass,
And I will be whole again.
My heart will be healed,
And I will be returned to the loving arms of grace,
Where I am fully embraced.

In the midst of life's heartaches, we must find the eyes to see beyond our current situation. The fact remains that we are going to have tough times. People are going to die. We are going to lose love. We are going to struggle. We can pray until we are blue in the face for things to be different, but most of the time we are powerless to stop heartache, because it is an inevitable part of life. Creation and destruction, life and death, good times and bad times . . . If you have a father who is riddled with cancer, there is probably a 99 percent chance that he is going to die. Praying for him not to, although you could do it, is a prayer that you can't expect God to answer. But what you can pray for, what you do have influence over, is for you to be the strongest, most centered and loving person possible during those times. You can pray for the courage to love through your fear, to allow love in through other sources. You can pray for enough love in your heart so you can grieve in a healthy way. You can pray for your loved one to find comfort, to have faith, to have an easy passing. What you do have power over, what you do need, is the understanding that this is life, that this too shall pass, and that an all-loving grace is with you and supports you in transcending the moment, enabling you to see beyond your current circumstances. The mantra "This too shall pass" lifts your consciousness so you can look at your life five days or five months out and know that you're going to be okay. Pain is inevitable. Suffering is optional.

Suffering, heartache, and agony come from our inability to process all our emotions. If we were to just let our fear be there without any resistance it would pass us by at some point, like a cloud floating by. If our anger were as welcome as our joy, it would be just a feeling inside us rather than an emotion that takes over our entire being. We would be able to be separate from it, observing its nature, observing ourselves, rather than becoming one with it. All the emotions that come our way at times of distress are there to teach us and guide us and give us the spiritual wisdom we need to move forward. But when we get caught up in all these emotions, become one with them, allow them to take over our thought process and our right to make conscious choices, we do the exact opposite of what wants to happen naturally.

Why do we do this? Because we take all our experiences so personally. We believe that the events of our life are somehow created and co-created by us, and because of this, we become attached to reality as we've known it, and we resist it changing. We become attached to the people in our life, our relationships, and the forms they take. We become attached to outer situations as well as inner states, and this attachment is what will ultimately cause us pain and suffering.

It's one of those cosmic paradoxes that, if we fail to understand, will trick us every time. We are to be open, loving, and inviting to situations, people, and experiences, but we must also be open to losing these same situations, people, and experiences. We could feel pissed off at God just for this alone. How is this fair? It seems like a setup, to be open to everything while knowing that at any time it may be ripped away from us. And since it is very human to hold on—it is in our genetic makeup to attach—it makes it even harder to let go. Just when we think we are doing fine, things change. People leave, die, and betray us. We lose a friend, a lover, a job, get taken for some of our earnings or get snubbed by a coworker. We lose our health, our energy, our dignity, and the elasticity in our skin. With each passing day we get closer to death, and all the drama of everyday life robs us of being present to what we have right now.

We must breathe into that. Ultimately we must reclaim our power to process challenging events so that we can move on. Yes, this is our opportunity and our challenge. Heartache will give us new life or it will speed up our internal death—the death of our dreams, our hopes, our joys, and our ambitions. We are in charge of this part of our life, and we get to choose.

Go ahead, choose. This is your opportunity. This is as good a time as any to say goodbye to any love you have lost in any form, whether a friend, a job, a lover, a family member, an opportunity, or an addiction.

> Dear God,
> May my awareness of what is
> Be more acute
> Than my memory of what was,
> May my love of what is

Be far deeper
Than my regret of what was.
Thank you for showing me the way,
Amen.

Breaking up is hard to do. But God can help us heal and support us in transcending the pain of our broken heart, if we let her.

Letting Go of Lost Love

I feel lost and alone without you, like a piece of me
has disappeared.

My heart aches for your touch.

I long for you to be near.

And even though I feel love for you,

Today I will summon the courage to let go of you.

I will let go of my dreams, my fantasies, and my regrets.

I will let go of the could-have-beens, the should-have-
beens, and the might-have-beens.

I will let go of my longing and my need to suffer over you.

I will let go of any and all negative attachments to you.

I will let go of my need to have you by my side.

Goddess of Love, I call on you now.

I know you have a greater plan for me

Even though I can't see it.

I know only you can fill the hole in my heart.

So I ask you today to please

Wipe away my loneliness

And wash away my tears

So that I may evoke the courage to cut the cords of
my aching heart

And replace them with strands of light that connect me to you.

Today I choose to trust in a power greater than myself.

To take away my loneliness and hurt, replace them with love and contentment.

Today I choose you, God, Goddess, as my lover.

I choose to think about you.

I choose to romance you.

I choose to seduce you.

And I choose to love you

Like I have loved no other.

I feel you in my body now.

I feel your love coursing through my veins.

I see myself soaring above my fear, above my pain, above my aching heart.

I feel you filling me up, dear God, and transporting me

To a place of love, peace, and contentment.

And so it is, and it is so,

Amen.

Holy Medicine

The Ultimate
Act of Self-Love

Forgive us our trespasses
As we forgive those who trespass against us.

Every day we must choose to forgive ourselves for our imperfections, for our conflicting desires, for our unhealthy impulses, for our judgmental mind, and our critical thoughts. We must choose forgiveness first in order to make peace with the aspects of ourselves and our life that we have ignored, neglected, abused, violated, betrayed, and hated—even in the subtlest ways. We must forgive ourselves for all our personal agendas and our righteous positions, which continue to lead us to believe that we are separate from the rest of the human beings in the world. Because when we are able to do this, we can choose to forgive all those around us. We can then see a bigger perspective, a grander version of our personal experience.

If you knew you were God, how would you treat yourself? How would you look at yourself differently? If you knew you held all of life's potential inside your heart, how would you view yourself right now?

There is nothing—and I mean nothing—that will give you more of what you want and need in life than forgiveness.

Forgiveness of self, of others, and of the world is what returns us instantly to our holiness. And for each one of us, forgiveness is a process. If we are committed to letting go of the past and ending the internal war, the steps to healing our hurt and anger will eventually lead us to "I'm sorry."

The love you can give to yourself today is to apologize and say "I'm sorry" for all the ways you've participated in behaviors and circumstances that didn't serve your deeper heart. This is a personal dialogue between you and the most private, delicate parts of yourself—an intimate conversation written for you and by you. This is where the healing needs to take place. It doesn't even matter if you intellectually understand why certain things will come into your awareness. It's about healing your emotional self and the shame you carry.

I'm Sorry

I'm sorry I didn't make better choices for myself.

I'm sorry I didn't take the time to make sure I was safe.

I'm sorry I stepped over my intuition and refused to listen to the messages of the universe.

I'm sorry I didn't ask for help sooner.

I'm sorry I allowed fear to guide so many of my choices.

I'm sorry I chose fear over faith.

I'm sorry I hurt people I love.

I'm sorry I couldn't make everyone understand my perspective.

I'm sorry I ever made this mistake.

I'm sorry I felt so desperate that I didn't take the time to do my due diligence.

I'm sorry I didn't have more faith in myself.

I'm sorry I hurt myself so badly.

I'm sorry I'm not perfect.

I'm sorry I couldn't see the bigger picture, and I'm very sorry I let others influence my decisions.

I'm sorry I wasn't wise enough to have worked everything out by myself.

I'm sorry I didn't know how to stand up for myself.

I'm sorry my heart was not strong enough and my ego
won out so many times.

I'm mostly sorry for the violence I did to my body and
psyche.

And with this, I ask all the sweet, scared, innocent parts
of myself to forgive me.

Once you express "I'm sorry" to yourself, you are finally clear
enough to offer a genuine apology to those around you whom you
might have hurt or who were hurt by observing your pain. Here
is one of my lists of apology:

*I'm sorry to all the people I have hurt directly and
indirectly.*

*I'm sorry for the pain others felt and for the powerlessness
they experienced just by being around me.*

*Please forgive me, my friends and loved ones, my family,
my coworkers, and my community.*

*To everyone who was on the opposing side of my conflicts,
please forgive me for all the ways you felt unloved,
disrespected, and uncared for by me.*

And lastly, you must apologize to your spiritual essence, the
part of you that wants you to have it all, be it all; the part of you
that suffers as you suffer, or at least shakes its head in disbelief as
you flounder around in your own private little hell.

For me, it was that I needed to apologize to God.

I am sorry to God for losing faith.

Please, God, forgive my unhealed heart and give me
the power and the courage now to forgive myself.

Self-Forgiveness

Dear God,

I have been so hard on myself.

I have carried the burden of everything I have done in my life that I regret.

I have shamed myself for all my imperfections.

I have shamed myself for doing too much and for doing too little.

I have shamed myself for being too flawed and for being so gifted.

I have shamed myself for the good I do and the good I don't do.

I have shamed others as I have shamed myself.

I have ignored my inner needs to serve others, to gain approval from outside myself.

I have sold my soul and stepped over my own boundaries to try to gain love and respect.

I have used others to try to fill up the deep hole that resides inside me.

I have made stupid choices, reactive choices, in an attempt to not be inconvenienced or feel the pain of right action.

I have tried to do it all on my own and have held unreasonable expectations for myself and others.

Today I ask that you support me in laying down the brutal bat that I use to beat myself up.

Today I acknowledge that when I beat myself up, I rob myself and others of the experience of my God-given gifts.

Thank you for the courage I feel right now to make the right choice,

The choice to forgive, to let go, to surrender, and to find compassion for my scared young child inside.

Today I choose to see the part of me that acts without thinking and speaks without questioning as the sensitive and terrified child she is.

Today I claim the power to re-parent this wounded child in a healthy and empowering way.

I choose to open my great, big, beautiful God-loving heart to her so that I may forgive her completely for all the sins of her past.

I forgive them and I forgive all of myself, now.

I feel myself letting go of all my self-induced torturous internal messages.

I hear solitude instead of noise.

I feel peace instead of heartache.

I feel gratitude instead of guilt.

I am free now.

I have chosen love over war.

I forgive and I am forgiven

I now stand with you as brave, bold, and fearless.

And so it is, and it is so,

Amen.

My Holy Heart

My holy heart, I offer you the love and compassion you deserve.

My holy heart, I give back to you all the energy I so generously put out to others.

My holy heart, I hold you as the sacred, precious jewel you are.

My holy heart, I am grateful for every feeling you experience, every pain that passes through you, every moment of joy and hope.

I love you like I love no other, because I know you are imbued with the richness of the universe and the light of God right now, inside me.

And when I embrace all of me, I will be able to love all of you.

I let go of old regrets and resentments from the past, and I become present with this radiant diamond in the center of my being.

And so it is, and it is so,

Amen.

Just breathe into that. You have a jewel. You are the jewel. Treasure yourself like a million pounds of gold. See and acknowledge your heart, and then notice what happens in the outer world. This is one of the most potent antidotes in existence for addressing the great pain in the heart of the world.

Forgiving God

I have suffered through many dark days,
Falsely assuming you had abandoned me.
My anguish and rage have clouded the truth,
But my precious heart still beats for you.

One of the biggest blocks to reconnecting and deepening
your trust in God is your ability to admit your anger and
disappointment toward the divine. So before you begin the
prayer for forgiving God, I want to encourage you to open up to
the possibility that you may, in fact, be angry at God.

Most of us were taught to fear God, not to hold God
responsible for the pains of our past. But I believe that most people
today are very angry at God. If you think about it, this makes
so much sense. What good is a God who is supposed to be there
for us, to answer our prayers, to protect us, to take care of us
in times of distress, and then doesn't show up? Most of us have
gone through so many hard and traumatic experiences, whether
we've suffered through addiction, health crises, molestation or
physical violence, or emotional abuse. We've been disappointed.
We've been let down. We wanted God to be there for us, but
she wasn't. We believe that the way God *should* have been there
for us was to shield us from these things happening to us in the

first place. But this is one of the hard, cold facts of life: God can't protect us from evil or from karmic experiences. Some things are simply meant to happen in order for our soul to grow and evolve. We need to have human experiences—including experiences of heartache and pain—in order to open up to the highest expression of ourselves.

When we don't look from a broader view at the wisdom of our human experiences, we naturally get angry at God. When we see all the suffering, all those who are going hungry, it's natural to be angry at a power we believe should be able to save us from these hardships. This anger is okay. We don't have to hide it. We don't have to beat ourselves up over it. We don't have to pretend it's not there.

I was blessed to see firsthand what happens when people allow themselves to express and then release their anger at God. Several years ago I had the honor of leading a three-day intensive Shadow Process workshop with my good friend and author of *Conversations with God,* Neale Donald Walsch. Neale loves to talk, so he did most of the talking, and I led most of the processes. We were a perfect match. The room we had rented for the weekend was in an old church in downtown La Jolla, California. We had brought our sound system with us to ensure that we had the music and the acoustics to deliver a powerful experience for those who participated.

On the second night of the workshop, I decided to lead the group in an anger process that always dramatically shifts people's lives. A little more than a hundred people were in the room, and we gave each person plenty of space and a blindfold so they could do the exercise safely and without being self-conscious about being watched by others. One crucial part of the anger process is the music we play. It's in four distinct stages of intensity; we play it very loudly, and it helps everybody get into the energy of all their unprocessed rage. Neale had already done a great job at introducing what we were going to do, including giving everybody permission to be angry at God, at least for the evening. I then took them through an internal process to open them up to all the times when they had thought God should have been there for them and wasn't and all their prayers that had seemed to go unanswered. By the time we were ready to start the next part of the process, I had the participants pretty pissed off. So we started the music and I was speaking loudly into the mic. People began doing some deep breathing—"chaotic breath," as it's called in the anger process. When it was time for people to let out their anger in words and screams, to voice out loud their rage, the music suddenly and inexplicably stopped. This is actually my worst nightmare because the music is so important to the process, and I half expected people to stop their catharsis when the room suddenly fell silent.

Instead, for the next twenty minutes, this group of a hundred or more screamed so loudly—crying, yelling, admonishing, and spewing their pent-up anger toward God—that nobody even noticed there was no music. The cries of pain and rage were so loud that we could hear nothing else. In all the years I've been leading the Shadow Process, five or six times a year, I've never witnessed such a powerful anger release.

When we finished, I asked everybody to find a place to sit or lie down on the floor. As they found a comfortable spot, I could still hear the sobs of many broken hearts. I then led the group in a forgiveness prayer. We began asking the all-loving presence to enter our awareness, to show us that she was there. By the next morning, there wasn't anyone in the room whose life hadn't been changed. No one could believe the amount of anger they had carried toward God. No one could believe the depth of rage they had experienced, and only a few could believe how great they felt after giving themselves permission to voice their anger at God.

Acknowledging our anger is the first step. Forgiveness is the step that sets us free.

Unburden Me

Dear God,

I have been very angry and disappointed with you.

There have been so many times when I needed you, and I don't believe you were there.

I have watched terrible things happen in the world, and horrible things happened to me that I believe you should have stopped.

My heart has been heavy with the anger I carry toward you.

My desperate pleas to you seemed to go unnoticed, my calls unanswered.

You left me when I felt I needed you most, and your perceived absence has robbed me of my faith and my connection to the universal good.

But today I acknowledge that you are by my side,

That you grant me greater understanding of how you work in my life.

Today I ask that I see the ways you have tried to show me you were there.

Today let me look through divine eyes rather than my small, individual eyes.

Let me see the ways you are in my life rather than focus on the ways you are not.

Let me know you as the loving grace you are.

Give me the understanding to know that you cannot save me from all the evil or pain I will meet, because this is part of the human experience.

Let me understand that love is your way and that I can always return to you for that love when I am scared.

Let me know that the power you are, and I am, can be tapped into each and every day, to give me the courage to face life as it is, not as I would like it to be.

Let me know without a shadow of a doubt that your love for me is real and that you will protect me through my instincts, inner urges, and outer roadblocks.

Let me recognize your gentle voice, like a nudge from a good friend.

Grant me the courage today to forgive you so I will have the ears to listen to you and the eyes to see you.

I powerfully choose to forgive you, God.

I love you and release my grudges now.

Thank you for your generous nature and for allowing me to express myself so completely.

I am now able to see beyond my narrow human perspective and understand that everything that has happened to me is ultimately serving me in becoming the grandest, greatest version of myself.

I accept that version now.

I gracefully allow my connection with you to strengthen so that I may know myself as the powerful force I am.

I feel it now, you and I together in the name of love, for the good of all people.

I thank you for this.

And so it is, and it is so,

Amen.

Here is another forgiveness prayer that my good friend Cliff Edwards, a longtime senior coach and trainer at the Ford Institute, wrote. I love it.

Dear God,

I stand exposed before you.

I ask for an outpouring of your wisdom, grace, and healing.

I invite you into my mind and heart so that I may return to the innocence of your love.

I need forgiveness, God.

My pain, loss, and righteous opinions have led me to be angry and hateful toward you.

In the light of your mercy and holiness I now open my heart.

I am sorry, God, for the judgments and profane thoughts I've held toward you.

For in my limited mind I know not the perfection and grandeur of your divine design for my life.

I ask for help to forgive and let go of my anger and blame.

And I ask for your forgiveness now so that I may receive your caring, guidance, and blessings every day.

I am forever moved and say thank you, God, for your miraculous, unconditional acceptance and forgiveness.

I choose now to be embraced in your peace and rest in your tender, loving arms.

And so it is, and it is so,

Amen.

Forgiving Others

Take away my grudges.
Take away my pain.
Release me of my hatred.
My heart is healed of blame.

Once we have forgiven ourselves and forgiven God, we are up
for the real task: to forgive others. Again I will quote my favorite
spiritual teacher, Emmet Fox: "When you hold resentment
against anyone . . . you are attaching yourself by a hook that
is stronger than steel." Now, would you want to be bound to a
person who has hurt you, betrayed you, lied to you, fucked you,
by something stronger than steel? How stupid would that be?
First they rip part of your heart out, and then you give the rest
of it to them? By clinging to your resentments, you rob yourself
not only of your power and peace of mind but also of your
connection to your holiness. It makes no sense. And don't think
you are hurting them with your grudges and resentments. Most
of these people *don't care* if you are hurt or angry; it's no skin off
their back. In fact, some people you hate are dead. So now you
not only don't have your power but you also have buried it alive
in someone else's grave. Crazy, right?

I've personally been through many difficult times in my
life. Some were definitely self-induced, and some were probably

karmic—in other words, unavoidable or meant to be. But no matter how they came about or whose fault they were—whether I created them or co-created them, whether I believed myself to be the victim or the victimizer—they are over now, and it no longer matters who was right or who was wrong, what they did or what I did. The only thing that matters is whether I can see the consequences of my actions or inactions and whether I've learned the lessons that these experiences have tried to bestow upon me.

There are a few questions that I always try to spend a sufficient amount of time dwelling on when I'm seeking the gifts that ultimately lead me to forgiveness:

How can I use this experience to become the kind of person my soul longs to be?

How can I use this lesson so that others can learn from me and maybe bypass a difficult life experience?

How can I use this incident to heal my heart?

How can I use this lesson to help heal the planet?

Believe me, when I'm angry or hurt, the last thing I want to do is ask these questions. Hurt and anger leave me feeling righteous and shut down. So first I have to heal the anger and the hurt, which is really the deeper invitation of the prayers in this section.

To begin, I have to give myself permission to feel, be with, and accept all the anger and hurt I'm carrying. I have to get out of my head, where I can justify and rationalize all my pain, and get into the heart of my inner child—the little sensitive part of me that likes to hold on to my pain as a form of self-protection. I have to, with open arms, give myself all the internal space I need to do the kind of healing work necessary to let go of the past, to forgive myself, and to forgive others. I have to acknowledge the aspect of myself that would rather hang on for dear life to my story, my position, my evidence, and my reasons rather than take responsibility and give up the blame.

By being willing to let go, I am fertilizing the ground of my consciousness, a necessity if I am to grow and move forward. It is the process of tilling the soil of my psyche and weeding the dead and useless emotional weeds so I can prepare my soul for new and exciting futures to emerge.

We only hold on to our resentments when we are still trying to prove we are right and the other person is wrong. Or when we are still trying to change what happened in the past or to gain a sense of control over our present circumstances. Maybe we still love the person, so we would rather be connected to them in a negative way than not to be connected at all. Or maybe they have become our excuse for why we don't have it all, for why we are stuck, or for why we continue to beat ourselves up. These are just a few of the reasons why we hold on to our resentments, but no matter what the reason, if we want to move on, to have a life greater than the one we have right now, we must forgive.

Just to be clear, you don't do this for the other person. You forgive for the sake of yourself. You do it for your freedom. Your resentments give others your power, your precious life force, your unlimited future. I recommend you take it all back and forgive. Next is a prayer that will make it far easier for you to do this.

Begin with the intention to heal your heart.

Cutting the Cord

Dear God,

With a heavy heart I come to you today, humbly asking your assistance to do what I have not been able to do for myself. I ask you to guide me and help me to forgive _____.

Today I admit to you and to myself that the resentment and rage that I hold against _____ is robbing me of an unencumbered future, a future filled with thousands of great possibilities that I am unable to see.

Today I am brave enough to admit that until I let go of the resentment against _____ I will always be dragging him/her with me everywhere I go, giving him/her my power, my peace, and my happiness.

Please, God, today let me know deep in my heart and soul that all things happen for a reason and even though I may not understand what that reason is right now, I trust you are looking after me and will provide me with wisdom and insight in your perfect time.

Please, God, let me see the blessings of what I have received and what I have learned from _____ so the pain in my heart will be transformed into gratitude and the confusion in my mind will turn to clarity.

Please grant me the courage I need to let the cords that bind me to _____ in negative ways unravel with ease and effortlessness.

Let me have the guts to cut the negative cords that continue to strip me of my self-esteem and bind me to _____.

Today please support me in saying goodbye, in transforming my hurt, anger, disappointment, and pain into lucky wisdom that will serve me in unimaginable ways in my future.

Please grant me peace with this person.

Thank you in advance for doing this with me.

Thank you for being with me in times of heartache and loss.

Thank you for filling my mind right now with the knowledge that I can do this.

Thank you for filling my body with the strength of courage.

With you, right now, I take back my power.

I see _____ standing before me with a humble face.

I see myself ten times bigger than _____.

I see the cords that have kept us tied together in negative ways,

And I see myself cutting those cords *now*.

And I say to _____, "I love you and I let you go forever.

"I forgive you and I release you now."

I see _____ floating away, getting smaller and smaller and smaller until he/she disappears from my view.

I breathe deeper now as I thank you, God, for I am free!

I now see one of the many gifts I will receive by choosing the bold and courageous act of forgiveness.

I am free, I am free, I am free.

Free at last, free at last, thank God almighty, I'm free at last!

And so it is, and it is so,

Amen.

As stated in *A Course in Miracles,* scribed by Helen Schucman and one of the most spiritual texts ever written, "The holiest of all the spots on earth is where an ancient hatred becomes a present love." Allow your holiness to dwell once again in the holy land of forgiveness.

An Evil Eye

God, watch over me.

God, protect me.

As I watch over

And protect myself.

The great question is, do we put our trust in God to keep us out of harm's way or do we take precautions to protect ourselves? There is an old Arabic story about a camel herder who, concerned about the safety of his flock, posed this question to the prophet Muhammad. "Great Prophet," he asked, "should I shackle the legs of my camels at night or should I have faith in Allah that they will be there in the morning?"

Muhammad's answer was both practical and wise. "Trust in God, *and* shackle the legs of your camel," he said.

In many cultures and for many people around the world, calling in divine protection is a part of their daily ritual. They might hang an evil eye near their front door or wear it as jewelry around their wrist. The intention of the red string worn by people who study Kabbalah is to guard against evil and protect oneself. It's an act of love to be responsible for ourselves, to guard ourselves against negative energies. We must be responsible for the energies that we allow in. Loving ourselves and honoring our instincts is a generous act of self-love, and it requires we be fully aware of, and trusting of, our instincts. We must open our eyes and see them as God's little nudges. When we pray for protection, it is the process of guarding our precious heart and our gentle soul.

There was a time when I didn't believe there was anything that we needed to be protected from except ourselves. And today I can honestly say I know that not to be true. There are people out there who want to harm others. There are people who want to take from others and who want what is yours to be theirs. There are people who are angry, jealous, envious, who feel less than you and want to be more than you, who want to get even with you. There are people you've hurt whom you didn't even know you hurt. Maybe when you met your husband, somebody else was in love with him. Maybe at the hair salon, while sharing about the grandeur of your family, you inadvertently opened the wound of someone who has lost love. When people take from you without regard, this is another wake-up call, requiring that you step into the next greatest version of yourself. This behavior, although it seems like it is against you, is nothing personal. And it is only when you are wounded that you make it so personal. Often the victim could have been any of a million other faces; unfortunately you just happen to be the one who got in their way. People without conscience or who victimize others feel entitled to take whatever they want even if it doesn't belong to them. This is just part of the human experience, and the biggest mistake any of us can make is to pretend this isn't so and to stay blind to the forces of evil.

There are many forces that show up through other people and that we need to be conscious of—not so we live a fearful, guarded life but so we are consciously aware, watching our own backs, so to speak, and so we have the presence of mind to call on all the powers that are available to help us. Calling on the divine powers of protection may support us in tuning in and listening to our instincts. It may help us to wake up the part of ourselves that already knows there are people who have bad intentions.

The prayer in the following chapter is designed to help protect you. It is a way to ensure you keep your eyes wide open on a day-to-day basis. This prayer will help you heighten your senses; you don't have to walk around with your back up, but if there is reason to be aware, you will become aware. This is a prayer you can say every day for protection.

Protect Me

Dear God,

I ask you, the angel of protection, my guides, my highest self, and any and all powers that be to protect me today.

I invite the part of me that is intuitively aware of my surroundings to be with me, guiding me today.

Please, God, cloak me with an impenetrable shield of light.

Watch over me today, and watch over my family and those whom I love.

Protect my precious heart, and give me the courage to see my enemy and do whatever it may take to guard myself against evil.

Angel of protection, guard me from those who minimize me, those who criticize me, those who seek to attack me, mentally, physically, or spiritually. I ask that your impenetrable shield of light surround me, and deflect and push back anyone who seeks to harm me and anyone who might be jealous or envious of me.

Today I ask the angel of protection to watch over me, guide me, and support me in being completely aware of my instincts and my intuition.

Allow me to know when to back away from somebody, to know when to open my heart and when to guard it.

Let me know when to lock my car, when to help a stranger, and when to seek refuge.

I thank you, God, for doing this for me. I thank my divine essence and the angels of protection for protecting my vulnerable heart, for shielding my sensitive spirit, for loving me enough and giving me enough courage to stand tall and strong, even when I'm terrified.

Today I see myself knowing who it's safe to be close to and who to stand back from.

Today I honor my amazing intuitive knowing.

Today I'm awed by the courage I have to trust my own instincts.

Thank you, dear God, for all of this. I feel your powers surrounding me now. I feel your shield of light covering me, protecting me, guarding me, and loving me.

I see any negativity bouncing off me and going right back into the earth, where it is absorbed.

And each time that happens, I see myself getting stronger, knowing that even with all expressions of my light, darkness may come again.

Today I choose to be responsible for protecting myself, for staying powerfully connected, and for having the courage to set strong boundaries.

Together with you, God, I say, "And so it is, and it is so."

Amen.

When you walk out the door, take a moment to be aware of your surroundings and be attuned to the people you interact with. Your job is to keep you safe, so always remember that God has blessed you with an internal barometer to help guide you and keep you safe.

Here is a quick little verse to use to evoke protection.

I am divinely loved and guided.

My divine instincts are finely tuned.

I am protected and safe.

I thank you, God, for watching over me and guiding me to watch over myself.

Reclaiming
Your Light

In Awe of the Potential of the Human Spirit

I'm standing in the greatest and grandest
version of myself.

I'm basking in the magic of the universe,

Drenched in the good vibrations of God's love.

Hallelujah, the light inside me is now on.

What does it take to step into and reclaim your holiness? I'm going to assert that it is much easier than you might imagine. Most of us think we have to become something, learn something, succeed at something, or achieve something, but in truth the realization of our holiest self requires nothing from the outer world. Stepping into our holiness is merely a process of acceptance, of being willing to see the totality of ourselves. It is the recognition of the magnificence and grandness of our potential.

In my first book, *The Dark Side of the Light Chasers,* I borrowed a metaphor from John Welwood's book *Love and Awakening,* in which he used a castle to illustrate the vast world that lies within us. Imagine that you are a magnificent castle with long hallways connecting to thousands of rooms. Every room in your castle is perfect and possesses a special gift. Each room represents a different aspect of yourself and is an integral part of the entire castle. As a child, you explored every inch of your castle without shame or judgment. Fearlessly you entered every room, searching for its jewels and its mysteries. Lovingly you embraced every room, whether it was a closet, a bedroom, a bathroom, or a cellar, knowing that each room was a unique and vital part of the place you called "home." Your castle was full of light, love, and wonder. Then one day someone came to your castle and told you that one of your rooms was imperfect, that surely it didn't belong in your castle. They suggested that if you wanted to have a perfect castle you should close and lock the door to that particular room. Because you wanted love and acceptance, you quickly closed off that room, and chances are, you never looked back. As time went by, more and more people came to your castle. They all gave you their opinions of your rooms, telling you which ones they liked and which ones they didn't. And slowly you shut one door after another. Your marvelous rooms were closed off, taken out of the light, and put into the dark. A cycle had begun.

From that time on you closed more and more doors for all kinds of reasons. You closed off rooms because you were afraid or rooms that you thought were too bold. You closed the doors to rooms that were too boring or too conservative. You closed doors because other castles you saw did not have a room like yours. You closed doors because your religious leaders told you to stay away from certain rooms. You closed any door that did not fit into society's standards or your own ideals about where you should live or who you should be. Like most of us, you may have locked away so many of your internal rooms that in time you forgot you were ever a magnificent castle, and you may have come to believe you are just a small two-bedroom house in need of repairs.

Now imagine your castle as the place where you house all of who you are, the good and the bad, the acceptable and the unacceptable, the beautiful and the ugly. One of the rooms in your castle represents love, one represents courage, one represents elegance, and another represents grace. There are an endless number of rooms in your castle, and every aspect that exists on the planet also exists within you. Creativity, honesty, integrity, health, assertiveness, sexiness, power, timidity, hatred, greed, frigidity, laziness, arrogance, sickness, and evil all occupy rooms in your castle. Each room is an essential part of the structure, and each room has an opposite somewhere in your castle. Fortunately, you are never satisfied with being less than what you are capable of being, and your discontent is the impetus, the little nudge that motivates you to search for all the lost rooms of your castle. You can find the key to your uniqueness and unlock the full potential of your holiness only when you make the courageous choice to open up all the rooms in your castle, removing the cobwebs, drawing the curtains, throwing open the windows, and letting the sunlight in again.

The castle is a metaphor to help you grasp the enormity of who you are. You may believe that you possess some positive traits and not others. But you are all things: what makes you laugh as well as what makes you cry. You are every beautiful and ugly trait rolled into one. It's vital that you seek out and find the light aspects of yourself that you have hidden away, because you can experience your holiness only when you're in the presence of the magnificence of all that you are. Then you will truly be in the presence of God.

The Bible proclaims, "The kingdom of God is within you." This kingdom is easily accessed if we are ready and willing to see the totality of who we are. Most of us are scared of what we will find behind the doors to the rooms we have locked away.

So instead of setting out on an adventure to find our hidden selves, full of excitement and wonder, we keep pretending the rooms don't exist. And the longer we deny and ignore the many unexplored chambers of our interior life, the more separation and loneliness we feel. Every one of us has countless rooms inside, and happiness comes to those of us who become dauntless explorers of the rooms in our souls. When we embrace the fullness of our humanity, we come face-to-face with our divinity.

Most of us are blind to the light that we are and the vast and mighty potential that we hold, because we have projected so much of our inner light onto other people. Projection is the unconscious act of transferring an aspect of yourself onto somebody else. But why attribute a portion of your light, your power, or your brilliance to another human being? Most likely because you were taught, from a very young age, that there was something inappropriate about some aspect of who you are. It happens so quickly, so simply. Somebody might have called you "stupid" when you were young, and you took that harsh word to heart, making it mean not just that you were stupid but also that *you weren't smart*. With that one unconscious decision, you unknowingly cut yourself off from the brilliant part of yourself—which we all have, by the way—and transferred it to someone you perceived as having a degree of brilliance that you did not. You may have heard the words "You're good for nothing" at some point in your childhood, and as a result you decided that you were unworthy of love or worth less than another. You then closed the door on your worthy self and instead went about collecting evidence that you are, in fact, unworthy. Maybe you were told to "be quiet" or "settle down," and as a result you disowned that big, fully self-expressed part of yourself, the part of you that has the guts and the courage to go out into the world and light people up.

If you grew up with imperfect parents or imperfect teachers or religious leaders with big agendas, I am certain you were made wrong more than once for expressing parts of yourself. So you opted for a course of action you hoped would preserve the love and acceptance of those around you: You hid these aspects. You squelched them. And you closed the door on them.

Most of us were taught not to acknowledge our greatness, lest we be perceived as vain or conceited. We may have been told to restrain our sexuality, our creativity, or our boldness as well, and we became afraid that these aspects might make others feel insecure. As a result, we express only a fraction of our true potential. The rest remains hidden in the recesses of our light shadow, hidden from others and also hidden from ourselves. As with the creation of the dark shadow, we subconsciously distance ourselves from many of our deepest gifts until we no longer recognize them as our own.

I Am That

Sometimes the only way you become aware of the glorious aspects of yourself that you've locked away is when you see them reflected back to you. In fact, one of the best ways to glimpse your own greatness is to look outside yourself to see who you deem as holy and to whom you have transferred your light. What if all the holy, enlightened spiritual beings who have lived throughout the ages, like Buddha, Jesus, and Gandhi, are merely reflecting back to you the potential of your human spirit? What if they lived to show you the vastness of your divinity, to model for you what's possible when you stand inwardly unified, accepting and loving of all of who you are? You claim another degree of responsibility for your life when you take back your light. There's no more whining, story, or excuse, because you are declaring, "I am that. I am that which I see in you." It's important to realize that all the people you project your light onto already have enough light. They don't need your light. *You* need your light. As Alan Cohen says in his book *The Dragon Doesn't Live Here Anymore,* "Great masters neither want nor need your worship. Your greatest gift to them and yourself is to emulate their divinity by claiming it as your own."

The Buddhists have a trick they use for taking back a projection. They have you think about somebody you have a judgment about—in this case, somebody you have a positive judgment about—and imagine that this person is standing right in front of you. Now take your hand and hold it directly out in front of you. Point your index finger toward the person whom you judge as being brighter, more lovable, or somehow holier than you. In pointing your finger at what you love and admire in them, you have just identified an unclaimed aspect of yourself. As a human, you do not have the ability to see yourself unless you are looking in a mirror, but you are ingeniously designed to see yourself in another. What stands out when you look at another— whether it is positive or negative—is a reflection of yourself.

Let me show you how this works. Right now, if I were to think about somebody I love, who I'm deeply inspired by, who lights me up, turns me on, and impels me to be more, it would be Dr. Martin Luther King Jr. To take back the light projection that I have on him, I would first take a moment to think about what specifically it is I love about him. What qualities do I see in him that light me up? After reflecting on this, I see that it is Dr. King's fearlessness and courage that I find so inspiring. Having identified these qualities, I then imagine Dr. King standing right in front of me. I hold my arm out, point my finger directly at him, and say, "You are fearless and courageous." Then I look out at my hand and I see that one of my fingers is pointing at him but *three* of my fingers are pointing back at me. So what does this tell me? Dr. King is reflecting back to me my denied fearlessness and courage. To be holy is to acknowledge the whole of oneself. So I must reclaim these qualities in order to reclaim another level of my wholeness. I need to take ownership and claim these two qualities for myself, in myself. I must acknowledge that I too am fearless and courageous and willing to enter uncharted territories. I must acknowledge that I am expressing these qualities now by writing this book about prayer. It is outside my comfort zone. It takes courage to reveal this vulnerable, holy part of myself, which is often covered by a deceiving outer shell. And it doesn't even matter if some people already see me as being fearless and courageous, because it's not about anyone else seeing my light; it's about me seeing my light. I am the one who has to own it and claim it. I have to be willing to open that door to my castle. So I breathe into it, allowing myself to feel the fear of being fearless.

There are people, past and present, like the Dalai Lama or John F. Kennedy or Mother Teresa or Oprah, who shine their light so incredibly brightly on behalf of us all—those who serve humanity as a whole. And while most of us would not argue that these are great and heroic people, it's imperative that we understand they are also mirrors of our own potential. What we are drawn to and what lights us up in others exists within us as well. Of course my courageousness will show up differently from Dr. King's. But because I too am here to serve the collective, and because I'm committed to making a difference in the world, I am deeply drawn to developing within myself the courage that makes this possible.

The truth is we have the potential to be all that we see in others. If we didn't have that same potential, we wouldn't see those aspects we admire in others. Our eyes wouldn't notice them. That's why, when you and I look at the same person, we each see and admire different qualities in them. You see your unclaimed light, and I see mine. We are only seeing ourselves. As long as we deny the existence of certain traits in ourselves, we continue to perpetuate the myth that others have something we don't. When we love, admire, or feel inspired by someone, it's an opportunity to find yet another buried aspect of our holiness.

Whenever we are in awe of someone, it's a clue that we are seeing in them some quality that we have shut off within ourselves. So as you look at holy beings like the Dalai Lama or Mother Teresa, or just people in your life whom you admire, try to distinguish the particular qualities they express that so inspire you. Are they unconditionally loving? Compassionate? Trusting? Tolerant? Powerful, kind, or generous? If so, you have just seen a part of yourself you have transferred to somebody else, a part of your holy self that you're not taking full ownership of. If you owned it completely, you wouldn't have to transfer it to anyone else.

If you see greatness, then it is *your own* greatness you are seeing. Close your eyes and really think about this. *Whenever I admire greatness in another human being, it is my own greatness I am seeing.* You may manifest it in a different way, but if you didn't have that same quality of greatness within you, you wouldn't be able to recognize that quality in someone else. If you did not possess that quality, you would not be attracted to it. Everyone sees other people differently because everyone is projecting different aspects of him or herself. In a seminar, I can ask a hundred people to tell me what qualities they most love or respect about the great icons of our time—people we all have a strong recognition of—and I'll hear forty different valued traits that people ascribe to each one of them. For example, with Paul McCartney, I'll hear "artistic genius," "musical pioneer," "adorable," "resilient," "trailblazer," "youthful," "loyal," "brilliant," "prolific," and more. About Oprah, I'll hear words like "magnificent," "magical," "generous," "compassionate," "funny," "strong," "authentic," "dignified," "spiritual," "powerful," and "visionary," just for starters. Of course there are those who project negative traits on them as well, but we're focusing on the light now. (If you want to discover the gifts of your dark side, I recommend reading my book *The Dark Side of the Light Chasers.*) Ultimately, it's your job to distinguish what holy attributes you are inspired by in other people and then reclaim those aspects of yourself that you have given away.

Until you are able to retrieve the light you have projected onto others, it will be impossible for you to experience the totality of who you really are. Your soul yearns to realize its full potential, to claim all its greatness, but only you can allow this to happen. Desperation comes from the gulf between God and self. To remember that you are one with all is to reawaken the God within you.

This conversation about reclaiming your light would not be complete without including the spectacular passage in the following chapter, written by spiritual teacher and author Marianne Williamson.

Letting Your Own Light Shine

Our deepest fear is not that we are inadequate,
our deepest fear is that we are powerful beyond
measure. It is our light, not our darkness, that
most frightens us. We ask ourselves, who am I to
be brilliant, gorgeous, talented, fabulous? Actually,
who are you *not* to be? You are a child of God. Your
playing small does not serve the world. There is
nothing enlightened about shrinking so that other
people won't feel insecure around you. We are all
meant to shine, as children do. We were born to
make manifest the glory of God that is within us.
It's not just in some of us; it's in everyone. And as
we let our own light shine, we unconsciously give
other people permission to do the same. As we
are liberated from our own fear, our presence
automatically liberates others.

—MARIANNE WILLIAMSON,
from A Return to Love

When you acknowledge the aspects of yourself that you've
disowned, you can begin the process of reclaiming them
through prayer. These prayers will support you in owning,
acknowledging, embracing, and expressing all of your divine
light. They will give you the courage to open each and every

door of the magnificent castle that is your higher self. They will coax the holy aspects of you out of hiding and liberate the untapped potential you've kept hidden from yourself and from the world. As you recite these prayers as part of your daily practice, ask God for the willingness to glimpse your own magnificence, unmasked and in all its glory. The reclaiming of these holy aspects of yourself, whether they are "compassionate," "grateful," "self-expressed," or "abundant," is the exact process that will return you home, that will help you take back your light. In the presence of your true self, you will fall in love with your whole self. As the poet Rumi said, "By God, when you see your beauty, you'll be the idol of yourself."

Reclaiming Your Light

Dear God, Goddess, Creator of All That Is,

Today I close my eyes and invite into my conscious awareness all the holy parts of myself that have been hidden from my sight.

I affirm that it's safe to open up to my deeply spiritual essence, to discover the divine thread that connects me to everyone else, seen and unseen, on the planet.

I proclaim that it is safe to come face-to-face with my greatness, my gifts, my spiritual vastness . . . my holiness.

Today, God, grant me the courage to stand without apology in the presence of all my greatness.

Give me the insight to reclaim the light that I've attributed to or projected onto others.

Allow me to open up and see what's possible for humankind when I stand fully in the presence of my holiness.

Support me, please, in being present to the importance of my own holy self.

Wash away anything that's between me and that divine thread, my divine essence.

Allow me to be humble enough to know that I have nothing to do with how divine I am.

Today, dear God, allow all the light that I've transferred out into the world, to people I know and to people I don't know, to people who are alive and to people who have passed, to return to me.

Bring all that light, right now, back into me.

Let me open my arms, my heart, to the uniqueness of my humanity and the magnificence of my divinity.

Let me know the divine as myself.

Holy Inspiration

Uncork the limitless flow of heavenly wisdom.

Let the divine influence pour forth from the depths
of my soul.

Let me drink the magical ambrosia of God's love,

As I am inspired to reach new heights.

Inspiration is magical, ever-present, and unlimited—you only
have to tap into it. You don't have to become inspired. You *are*
inspired. Beyond all limitations of human life, inspiration is the
emanating force of the universe. It lives vibrantly in the present
moment, when you are connected to God and know yourself
and God as one, when you step outside your intellect, your
mind, your emotions, and your ego. Inside your ego structure,
you can be excited, motivated, and even driven, but that is not
inspiration. Inspiration comes from the invisible world, bringing
spirit into matter. You just have to reach up and pull it down.

There have been many times when I've been leading a
workshop or giving a lecture and simultaneously going through a
challenge in my personal life—stuck, trapped, locked inside my
ego's pain. But with hundreds of people waiting to participate with
me to transform some aspect of their lives, there's no time for me
to dwell on my personal issues. Instead I have to go *beyond* them,
I have to reach up and pull God in. I have to step outside the

smallness of my individual self and tap into the collective pool of higher consciousness. In this sacred pool is all the inspiration any one of us could ever want. Inspiration is the spiritual fuel of a divinely connected life.

To access inspiration, all you have to do is melt away whatever worry, concern, thought, or belief is keeping you separate from the level of consciousness where inspiration resides. Inspiration is a vibrational frequency. You have to make the choice to stop doubting yourself and your connection to God. You have to give up your need to feel small and invisible. You have to hand over your resignation, your meekness, your inadequacy, and give up being stuck. You have to give up the idea that you don't have it or don't know how to access it. And you have to hand over all your small, disconnected thoughts to the Goddess of Inspiration. When you are no longer clinging to the thoughts of your ego, you are free to step into the power of your love and the brilliance of your being. As you say the following prayer, imagine calling forth the Goddess of Inspiration. I envision her as a beautiful woman, light, airy, passionate, and absolutely self-expressed. Give her permission to reveal herself to you, to move through you and to guide you.

Unleashing Your Inspiration

Dear Goddess of Inspiration,

Please bless me with your presence today.

Allow me to look through your big, beautiful wide-open eyes,

The eyes that see my goodness and know my greatness,

The eyes that invite the miraculous to occur,

The eyes that dance with the magic of the universe.

Goddess of Inspiration, allow me to rise above my fears, doubts, concerns, and day-to-day dramas so that I may step into your magical, pulsating energy field of inspiration.

Allow anything other than my most inspired moments to melt away, to be removed ... to drop off me like a loose piece of clothing.

Tell me what I need to let go of today in order to merge with you completely in this moment.

Give me the opportunity to stand fully present with all that is available to me today.

Allow me to feel the ecstasy that is possible for me today.

Allow me to see what hearts I can touch today.

Allow me to hear the words I can communicate, write, and think today that would uplift me and all those around me.

Goddess of Inspiration, surround me with your golden, beautiful, warm, tingly light, and allow me now to step into my most inspired self.

I claim it. I choose it.

I commit to you now, to walk as my most inspired self, to talk as my most inspired self, to create, to give, to love, to parent, and to work as my most inspired self, always drawing upon your energy as my fuel.

I claim now that I am all I can see, and because I can see you, Goddess of Inspiration, I am you.

Thank you, God, Goddess, and all the powers that be, for blessing my heart, quieting my mind, and igniting the passion in my soul.

I am one with you, and with you, I say, "And so it is, and it is so,"

Amen.

Before you say the prayer in the following chapter, think about a goal or a desire, something that you've been wanting, that you've been asking for, that you have a deep desire to experience. Now is the time to ask for the inspiration to call it into being. Then get comfortable in your prayer seat, take a few slow, deep breaths, and speak this prayer out loud.

Inspiring Creation

Dear God,

In this moment, I open up all that is inside me so that I may be moved, inspired, and connected to something bigger than myself.

I humbly admit that I've been unable to manifest this desire inside the confines of my ego structure.

I confess to you now that I don't know how to do it and that I can't do it alone.

I affirm my connection to that miraculous power that exists inside and outside me, the all-knowing, ever-loving force that sustains me and brings me the fulfillment of all my desires.

I ask the powers that be to join me, to align with me and my highest self, and I invite my ego and my lower self, my fear and self-doubt to relax, to be soothed and embraced by the warmth and the grandness of my holy self.

I ask all parts of me, all aspects of me, to come into alignment with the fulfillment of my desire.

I now declare my desire out loud,

And my words are lifted into the realm of consciousness where my dreams are turned into reality.

Thank you for this.

And so it is, and it is so,

Amen.

Holy Expression

Grant me the courage to speak my truth.
Give me the strength to sing my praises.
Bless me with the confidence to let my voice be heard.

When we allow the well of inspiration to open up inside ourselves, we are gifted with the reconnection of our most expressive self. Each of us has a voice, a great, big, beautiful voice that has a rhythm and a resonance unlike any other. This voice can express itself through any number of channels. It may be with words, with art, with photography, with dance, with cooking, with music, with kids, or with work.

Your unique voice is strong, clear, and a contribution to your world. So often I hear people say, "I am stuck. How can I get unstuck?" But to be "stuck" is to be in a trance inside your ego. Once you are awake, stuck no longer exists. It is replaced by the unlimited wellspring of divine consciousness.

Call on the source of all expression to visit you, open you up, and reveal to you all that you are and all that wants to be expressed through you at this time. Don't try to force it, push it, or make it come. Instead, coax it, seduce it, invite it to come through you now. Here is a lovely prayer written by my good friend and former senior staff member of the Ford Institute Donna Lipman. This is a woman who found her voice in the

Shadow Process and has literally transformed thousands of lives since.

> Dear One at the Source of My Being,
>
> I welcome you in this moment with a grateful and loving heart.
>
> I greet you with joy and wonder, and I bless you for your gift of divine guidance.
>
> I call upon my body, mind, and soul to be open to the healing only you can impart.
>
> I pray that the gift you have bestowed upon me of ingenious purpose be shared and fulfilled.
>
> I pray for my total freedom and freedom for all beings in this world.
>
> I pray to be a worthy inheritor of your creative spirit and a divine guide for others.
>
> Thank you for gracing me with bold, outrageous self-expression.
>
> Thank you from every cell of my being for the ability to cry out loud and laugh out loud.
>
> Thank you for guiding me to my truest and fullest self; I revel in singing skies and dancing waters.
>
> Knowing I am safe and protected by your love, I passionately sing your praises from the highest mountaintop.
>
> For so it is, and it is so,
>
> Amen.

The Holy Elixir

Let me be God's alchemist.
Let me turn water into wine,
Mud into gold,
And my wounds into wisdom.
Let me know a grateful heart.

There is nothing better than a grateful heart, a heart filled with appreciation, joy, love, humility, and a dash of openheartedness; it's the perfect elixir. This perfect elixir is an alchemical potion to ensure good health, vitality, passion, and pleasure. This life-affirming, blood-enriching potion gives us a direct line to divine consciousness. The blissful feelings of gratitude and appreciation provide us with sweet confirmation that we are in alignment with our highest self.

Don't you love it when you have a grateful heart? Whenever I'm present to all the gifts that surround me—whether it's a glimpse of the beautiful Pacific Ocean; a giant black crow flying by my window; the perfect mix of turkey, sweet potatoes, stuffing, and gravy in one scrumptious forkful; or an evening with my favorite spiritual teacher, Ammachi, singing, chanting, praying, and meditating—life seems so easy, so precious, so plentiful. All of that, along with a special smile from my son, and the only words left to say are "Thank you." In the attributed words of the great German mystic Meister Eckhart, "If the only prayer you ever say in your whole life is 'Thank you,' that would suffice." "Thank you" just may be the holiest words you ever utter.

Stirring Up
the Holy Elixir

Dear God, Goddess, and any and all powers that be,

Thank you for showering me with your divine grace and filling me with your boundless inspiration.

Thank you for my ability to receive and express all of my light and to learn and extract the wisdom from my darkness.

Thank you for all the amazing people you bring into my life, with whom I share love, laughter, wonder, and purpose.

Thank you, God, for all that is waiting to be explored and manifested by me in this coming year.

Thank you for all the love that I find inside and outside me.

Thank you for your heartfelt presence.

I am yours, and you are mine.

You are my beloved, and my beloved is me.

Today I choose to live with you as my partner, dear God.

I choose to be the kindest, most loving and creative expression of you that I can possibly be.

I choose to show the world around me what's possible when we make the choice to partner with you and to live the grandest, greatest version of ourselves.

May you grant me today the freedom to give up my small, doubt-filled, fearful self and infuse me with the courage to embrace the grandness of my most magnificent self.

Thank you, God, for granting me the power to create and co-create with you, time and time again.

May I joyfully surrender and gracefully express your will, always.

And so it is, and it is so,

Amen.

The Appreciative Heart

Dear God,

Thank you for giving me my body, my hands, my feet, and my heart.

Thank you for all the people who are in my life, and thank you for giving me the ability to love, care for, and contribute to others.

Thank you for allowing me to grow and evolve, to shed the old and make room for the new.

Thank you for my ability to see new opportunities and to explore new paths.

Thank you for giving me the ability to think for myself and, more importantly, to make wise choices.

Today I give thanks for my right to choose new perspectives, new beliefs, new interpretations, new behaviors, new habits, and a new attitude—all God's gifts to me, all free, all accessible at any moment.

Thank you, God, for waking me up to how truly blessed I am.

May the love that fills my heart right now go out and enter into the hearts of all the people who are seeking it—the ones I know and the ones I don't know.

May your will be done in all things.

And so it is, and it is so,

Amen.

Heart Candy

Heart candy is self-acknowledgment at the deepest level. It's honoring who we are and what we do every day rather than taking it for granted. It's taking time out at the end of the day to say to ourselves, silently or aloud, "Wow, look at me. I volunteered for an hour at the school. I cleaned the kitchen. I did my taxes. I washed my car. I called my grandmother to check in even though I didn't feel like it." We give ourselves heart candy when we acknowledge the effort it takes to be a human being. Most of us believe that we should just do the things we need to do—why should we honor or thank ourselves? But our deeper self yearns to be acknowledged for every step we take toward goodness. Self-acknowledgment allows us to feel deeply connected to God, and when we acknowledge ourselves we acknowledge the greater whole.

I remember a time in my life when I was absolutely exhausted from flying all over the country, leading workshops and lecturing. My friend Justin was with me one night and he could see how depleted I had become. He said to me, "I want you to treat yourself like you are Ammachi. I want you to treat yourself like you would treat a holy and sacred and important being." Immediately I felt my resistance. "But I'm not her," I said. "She's special. She's holy." And of course the moment those words left my lips I saw that I am her. We're all her. She is just a beautiful, clear mirror who reflects back to us our own divinity.

Ammachi is a piece of the divine, as we all are. Giving yourself heart candy acknowledges this fact. It's a way to treat yourself like the special, loved, honored being that you are. And when you love yourself in the privacy of your inner world, you create, draw, and magnetize love to yourself in the outer world.

So how do you give yourself heart candy? The easiest way is to take notice of how you would like other people to treat you, what you'd like other people to say about you, what you'd like other people to think about you, and then interact with yourself like that. If you want people to respect you, treat yourself with the utmost respect. If you long to be appreciated by those around you, then appreciate each and every thing you do each day. If you'd love for other people to notice and acknowledge your brilliance, then you acknowledge your brilliance. If you want others to be loving and compassionate toward you, then be loving and compassionate toward yourself. Open your heart to you. Think the sweet thoughts that make you smile. Say the words to yourself that your heart longs to hear. Practice sweet gestures and acts of kindness toward yourself.

I have spent a lot of time thinking about addiction. Whatever we're addicted to, whether it's alcohol or sugar or sex or drugs, it's because we are craving some sweetness. I believe we reach for our addictions when our inner world and our human heart are craving nurturing, goodness, and acknowledgment. So many of us had tough childhoods, but the truth is, in every moment we have the opportunity to re-parent ourselves. We have the opportunity to reprogram ourselves with some heart candy, to create a new imprint on our heart. The process begins at home, inside us. If we can't give sweetness to ourselves, if we can't feed ourselves, nothing else will taste sweet enough. People can shower us with all the love in the world, but if we don't love ourselves, we won't be able to receive it.

In my coach training program people are led through a process where they stand in circles and whisper in one another's ears all the things they longed to hear as a child: "I'm so happy you're here." "I've never seen a more beautiful being than you." "I'm going to care for you like I've never cared for anybody." "You're so special." "You're unique." "You're beautiful." "You're talented." "I love you." What do those words, and the energy that is encoded within them, do when they enter your heart? Heart candy is actually food for your soul. Remember, the outer is a reflection of the inner world. If you want your outer world to shift, you need to do nothing more than begin treating your inner world in a whole new way, in a holy way.

Most of us treat ourselves so much worse than we would ever treat another human being. We withhold love, appreciation, fun, rest, and acknowledgment from ourselves. Is it any wonder, then, that we have cravings? What we think we're craving from the external world is an illusion. We will only find it from the heart candy we give ourselves.

Feeding ourselves heart candy is how we encode our consciousness with the experience of our holiness. It's how we lift up out of the gravitational pull of the world around us, time and time again, and remind ourselves of who we truly are.

Heart Candy Prayer

Today I take a moment to imagine what would be possible if I reclaimed my holiness.

How will I treat myself, knowing that I am a holy being?

Who will I choose to have around me, knowing that I am a holy being?

How do I feel in my body when I acknowledge the depth of my holiness?

Tell me now, God, the words that I need to say to be in the presence of my holiness.

The universe is on my side.

I have everything that it takes.

I am loved and adored and cherished.

The world is just waiting for my greatness.

Life is fun and easy.

The whole world is my cheerleader.

I am brilliant.

Life gives me everything I need.

Oh my God, I'm doing such a fabulous job.

I love how brave I am.

I love how loving I am.

I am majestic.

I acknowledge myself for all that I am and all that I've done.

I am an amazing person.

I'm in the right place. I'm in the right time.

I am a divine, holy person.

I have the right to experience everything magical in this world.

My heart is so filled with love and compassion.

The hard part is over. The good times are here!

It's time for me to open up and enjoy.

Hurray for me! I did it.

It's my time to have more belly laughs than I've ever had in my life.

My smile is brighter.

I am open to a greater level of love and intimacy and partnership and friendship with all the people in my life.

I have a beautiful heart that lights up the world.

I am a brilliant person who is making a huge difference in people's lives.

My presence is a blessing.

I am an absolutely enchanting and magical human being. I adore myself.

I am as delicious as a chocolate truffle.

As I say these words, I allow them to penetrate every cell in my body. I open my heart and feel the presence of all my greatness.

Give me the courage to be respectful of my gifts by using them to their fullest.

Give me the freedom to let go of anything that's in the way of me expressing my gifts.

I love you, God. And I know that by loving you, I love all of me.

And together with you, I say, "And so it is, and it is so."

Amen.

Now is the time to open yourself up daily and feed yourself the love and nourishment you've been looking for.

Shower Me with Love

Refresh me with your morning dew.

Shower me today with sweet thoughts and tender feelings.

Let me feel deep inside the love I have for you and the love you hold for me.

Fill my mind with thoughts of goodness and grace, warmth and connection.

Let the sprinkle of hope penetrate my heart and stillness permeate my mind.

I am an instrument designed for you, my Lord, to use in the ways you deem necessary to make my world a better place.

I wish to bring joy to the joyless, hope to the hopeless, and love to the loveless.

Today let me be reminded of how important I am.

Let me know that my life matters.

Let me feel how all that is good and all that is great await me in this beautiful new day.

I thank you in advance for every sign of goodness you bring into my awareness.

I thank you for all that I am and all that I will become.

I thank you for showing me the way with grace and ease and for always being with me, in good times and in bad.

I thank you for opening me up today to new experiences, deeper joy, and unimaginable amounts of appreciation.

Today I choose to turn my will over to you and a higher purpose.

Together with you, I say, "And so it is."

And because we are one, I say, "And it is so."

Amen.

Holy Commitment

In this life and beyond,

With every breath I take,

With every word I utter,

With every choice I make,

With every twinkle of my soul's light,

I promise to share the never-ending,
shining love that I am

With all beings, everywhere,

Forevermore.

Reclaiming your light is a holy commitment you make, not only to yourself but also to everyone around you. It is the commitment to keep choosing the high road, to keep reminding yourself that you are the light, the brilliance, and the beauty that you see in others. It's the commitment to crack open shell after shell of the person you have been in the past and to trust that what will be revealed is in God's highest plan for you. It's the commitment to take step after step into the unknown, trusting that there is a higher power and a higher plan that will be there to hold you. And even if you fall, there will be someone there to catch you.

What is the holy commitment you want to make to yourself now in order to acknowledge the light of who you are? What images will you feed yourself? What structures will you put in place around yourself? What people and environments will you surround yourself with? What will you do to encode your consciousness with the experience of God? More importantly, how will you remember that you are the one who dictates the level of consciousness that you live in?

What commitment to yourself, to your holiness, will pop you out of bed in the morning and right into your prayer seat, where you can connect with the invisible force that is at the source of your being? What would you have to be committed to that would radically alter your life and fill you up with what you are looking for? It's not going to be losing ten pounds or making more money. You've done that. You've planned a year, set goals, you've had successes, and yet still there is something missing. Why is this? It is simple and it is obvious, yet you always need to be reminded, because what you are looking for does not exist outside you. It does not exist in some project or person. All that is temporary. What your soul is longing to experience, to have and to hold, is your birthright. It's free, it's peaceful, it's always there. It's unable to betray you, unable to leave you. You can leave it, but it will never leave you. It can't die. It can't pass out on you. It's like the air you breathe . . . It's your connection with God, your God self, your holiness. Waking up and servicing this part of your life is the only guarantee that you'll ever have all the love, peace, happiness, and fulfillment you long for. This is not a joke, nor is it a trick. It is the universal truth. It is the only promise of unconditional love that can be kept, that can never be broken no matter what you do. You can ignore it, hate it, call it names, abandon it, betray it by playing on the dark side of life, and close the door on it, and it will still be there for you.

What you are seeking at the deepest level exists inside you, in the quietude of your inner world, in the privacy of your sweet heart. So now it's your responsibility, your holy responsibility, to encode your consciousness with thoughts, feelings, and images that will support you in creating the perfect internal environment to cultivate a deep and intimate relationship with the one you call God. This is the force that loves you, cheers for you, and wants it all for you. In a world where love leaves as quickly as it comes, you can rest now, knowing that you have found a love that will never misguide you and never leave you. My advice, dear friend, is to take great care of that love. It will give you everything you've been looking for.

Each and every time you experience that holy shift in consciousness—however it happens—it's vital that you acknowledge it with "I did that." You are the only one who can choose. You are as free to change vibrational frequencies as you are to change your clothes. Your thoughts, your emotions, the images you hold in your mind, the energetic signals that you send out to all those around you—these are the tools that are available to you in this life experience. Use them to your full advantage. Do not for one more minute deny your holiness, your godliness, and the power of your true self. Because you are wanted, needed, and, more importantly, a holy addition to this world. So open up, commit, and enjoy this journey, your holy ride.

ABOUT THE AUTHOR

© Miklos Szabo

Debbie Ford was an internationally recognized expert in the field of personal transformation and a pioneering force in incorporating the study and integration of the human shadow into modern psychological and spiritual practices. She was the executive producer of *The Shadow Effect* movie and personally led thousands of people from around the world through her renowned Shadow Process Workshop. She was the founder of The Ford Institute, where she supported the highest expression of those people who wanted to make a difference in the world. She was the *New York Times* bestselling author of nine books; *Your Holiness* is her tenth. Debbie died of cancer on February 17, 2013, but her legendary work lives on.

www.debbieford.com

DEBBIE FORD'S
LEGACY LIVES ON!

If you connected with the prayers and sentiments shared in this book and want to continue being elevated by the eloquence, infused with the faith, and awakened by the wisdom of this amazing thought leader and teacher . . . there is more.

Debbie's work lives on at The Ford Institute.

The Ford Institute was founded by Debbie in 2000 to teach life-altering tools, skills, and concepts to empower you to see through new eyes, act in new ways, step into new possibilities, and create a life beyond your wildest dreams.

The mission of The Ford Institute is to liberate you from the prison of your past and the confines of your negative thoughts, limiting beliefs, and self-sabotaging behaviors. This work, as poignant and powerful today as it ever was, guides you to embrace a life of authenticity, abundance, and unprecedented feelings of confidence, gratitude, and love.

We invite you to come explore The Ford Institute's offerings including personal development courses, a professional coaching training, corporate programs, and the absolutely unparalleled live Shadow Process Workshop, which was Debbie's signature work and is known as being one of the top transformational workshops!

When Debbie appeared on Super Soul Sunday with Oprah Winfrey in February of 2012, she said,

> *"If I could, I would take the whole world through The Shadow Process."*

If you want to continue being Drenched In Holiness and the brilliance of Debbie Ford, visit www.TheFordInstitute.com/YourHoliness to receive even more gifts from her life-changing legacy.

It's time to bask in the light of your magnificence and dance in the delight of liberation and possibilities!

HAY HOUSE

Look within

Join the conversation about latest products, events, exclusive offers and more.

 Hay House UK

 @HayHouseUK

 @hayhouseuk

 healyourlife.com

We'd love to hear from you!